CELEBRITIES WHO HAVE MET ME

A CHILD OF THE LOST EMPIRE

Publisher: Adagio Media.
Website: Celebritieswhohavemetme.com

Creator: D'Eathe John, Vancouver, author.
Publication editor: Kevin McDonald.
Title: Celebrities who have met me. A Child of the Lost Empire.

ISBN: 978-1-9994339-2-5
Subjects: Contemporary historical memoir. Political and social commentary.
Cover design: Emily Rose.

CELEBRITIES WHO HAVE MET ME

A CHILD OF THE LOST EMPIRE

JOHN D'EATHE

Published by Adagio Media

Meet the Author

John D'Eathe was educated in the United Kingdom in law and urban land economics. After training in the City of London he set off blithely for an adventurous business life in Colonial Hong Kong and Asia. A decade later he returned to England but moved on to Canada, commencing a long career in major property investment and development throughout North America and in various parts of the world. He traveled extensively and witnessed the various cultural subtleties of getting things done. He and his wife Lane live in West Vancouver and enjoy visiting their widely located family and friends.

Contents

At its peak, in 1919, after winning the First World War, Britain had the largest empire in history and for more than a century had been the leading global power. I was a proud Child of that Empire!

Indoctrination

By the outbreak of the Second World War in 1940, a few years after I was born, the British Empire still included a quarter of the world's population and a fifth of the land mass.

Most of its original subject countries were still under its control at this point, although they had already relinquished the United States of America, Canada, Australia, Newfoundland, New Zealand, South Africa, Afghanistan, Ireland, Egypt and Iraq.

I was a Child of that Empire, and we were under attack.

Little Lord Benjie Guinness

Commanding my deadly military platoon, I crept along a hedgerow.

The dastardly Hun attacked. "Open fire!" I shouted and we stood, defiant in fearless bloody combat, mowing them down to a man.

We hunted every day for the hated *Adolf Hitler,* but the most infamous celebrity of all, the Fuhrer himself, was a no-show! He would not risk crossing the English Channel for fear of meeting me.

It was 1940, on the East Coast of England. Killing Germans was my daily duty, fiercely brandishing my prized Christmas present from Santa, a wooden, painted Tommy-gun, à la Al Capone. That gun stayed with me always, for protection of the Empire in the imminent invasion; even in bed where the unfortunate Hitler met me in my dreams.

Late in the 1930s, when war appeared to be imminent, then *Prime Minister Neville Chamberlain* had returned from a conciliatory visit to *Adolf Hitler*, assuring the British Empire of "Peace in our time".

This was to prove to be the most infamous and naive pronouncement of the century, although he apparently never actually said that. "Peace *for* our time," is widely reported to be what he said as he waved his useless signed paper. Not that it mattered, and thereafter my young life was plunged into war, with *Winston Churchill* growling in the background.

* * *

Little *Benjamin Guinness,* the future *Right Honorable, the 3rd Earl of Iveagh, Viscount Elveden, Member of the House of Lords,* was being delicately sponged down by his personal maid in the nursery at nearby stately Elvedon Hall.

A few miles away from Benjie, a slightly older chubby baby, John Death, was splashing happily in his little tin bath in front of a coal fire in a little grey brick house.

The building stood protectively back from the busy street and possessed a well-groomed front garden. In common with local homes, however, it had one cold-water tap in the kitchen, the only indoor plumbing. There was an outdoor privy, but no bathroom in the house and no central heating.

The tin bath hung on an outside wall to be brought in on Friday nights for the weekly family bathing ritual in front of the small coal fire in the sitting room. The tub was filled by bucket from the copper boiler in the out-house where the family laundry was washed by hand.

This was perceived as no hardship; it was normal living. Working folk in the United Kingdom all lived under similar conditions, even at the height of the wealthiest Empire ever. The 'one per cent' is not a recent concept!

Little *Benjie* was only twenty-five miles away, but it could have been a thousand! To him I would be a grubby little peasant.

His dad was Viscount Elveden and his grandfather was the grand *Earl Iveagh*, richest man in Ireland. Their English home Elvedon Hall was an enormous, stately mansion set in spacious parks, lording it over one of England's largest agricultural estates.

Benjie shared my birthdate, May 20, although he was born a couple of years later, in 1937.

My granny Sarah had essentially been a serf, her parents 'tied to the land' on such a Suffolk fiefdom. As a child she toiled in the fields 'picking stones' for a penny a day. But they survived, encouraged by the knowledge, that out there in Our Empire there were many poorer coloured folks who were far worse off.

Sarah did not rate any schooling, but Little Benjie was destined for Eton School and Cambridge.

Back in the 1930s, however, he soon ran out of luck, and they lost their Elvedon mansion when it was requisitioned by the US Army Air Force as their headquarters and then blown apart by enthusiastic German bombing. Benjie had long before been taken to the relative safely of County Kildare in Ireland.

* * *

"Call me Benjie!" he enthused, now Lord Iveagh, trying to establish a friendly relationship with me and thrusting a generous glass of wine into my hand. It was now 1972 in a Canada long free of his Empire domination, and he needed my help.

There we were, finally drinking equally together. It was to be the way of my life, being advanced by those celebrities and enabled by the final throes of the quickly depleting British Empire!

* * *

My first memory of those war days is literally a few weeks before it started. I was a toddler at the seaside with my parents and we were touring a moored ship. We were being shown the engine room with pounding machinery and my father, Bob, picked me up from the deck to look out of a porthole.

This lifelong memory had to be from the summer of 1939, just before the nearby seafront town Clacton was closed and its beaches barbed wired and fortified. I was four.

War with Germany was declared that September.

The frantic preparations for war on the East Coast of England were then actively going on around me and dominated those first years of my life.

Those problems in Europe were all being caused by three villains, you could consider celebrities, whose evil faces dominated my youthful dreams. Their fates emerged as I grew older.

The first was *Benito Mussolini* who was elected in 1922. He went on to grab the dictatorship of Italy, as Il Duce, forcing the issue with his paramilitary Black Shirts, and was to reign until his violent death just before the end of war.

He was closely followed by *Francisco Franco*, who skipped the niceties of election altogether and in 1936 gained the support of the army in the Spanish Revolution. It produced one the worst series of atrocities to that date. The civil war ran until 1939 with systematic killings, torture and all types of brutality, killing hundreds of thousands. He himself took a traditionalist view, supported the monarchy, the church, land-owners and order. He never swung widely in support of communism or fascism and was thus able to keep Spain as independent and out of the world war.

Third came my arch villain of all, *Adolf Hitler*, who like Mussolini was elected in the first place, in January1933, but was highly impatient and seized control of the country with his literally murderous Nazi Party force, the next year, having received the wholehearted support of the very rightwing army.

Hitler started flexing his military muscles in Europe, hence Chamberlain's appeasement visit in 1938.

In my early years these evil forces were drummed into my mind together with new heroes, Churchill, Roosevelt and Stalin; all reputedly good people!

Back there in the war, however, my Empire was under attack. The Hun were pounding us. Our windows were taped, everything boarded over. We piled defensive sandbags at strategic points and helped build real gun emplacements. But Hitler made the deadly mistake of not crossing the channel and our immediate concerns subsided.

German bombers were still droning overhead to bomb the interior industrial areas. On their way back, with American and British airfields nearby, they dumped their spare bombs on us, thump, thump, thump. I kept a wary young eye up to the sky and listened for the feared deep drone of the Messerschmitt engines, ready to take cover.

Dad shouted, "Down the shelter." Wrapped in our eiderdowns, and heeding the town's strident, wailing air-raid siren, we rushed into the damp corrugated iron Anderson Shelter which was buried in the garden, shivering as planes, friendly and foe, rumbled overhead. Then the calming steady sound of the All-Clear siren.

Later in the war came the droning Doodlebugs and then the more deadly V2 whooshing rockets. I lay in the shelter, looked up at the rusting iron structure and held my breath for their engines to falter, or cut out. They were launched randomly from Germany in our direction and eventually ran out of fuel to drop and blow up someone! Anybody!

But I had my trusty Tommy Gun, Churchill and the Empire. I would prevail!

* * *

Winston Churchill boomed defiance from our sole communication; the wireless.

My parents had crouched earlier, entranced, around that same radio, when the American celebrity, Orson Welles held them spellbound with his realistic report of a Martian invasion in his dramatisation of War of the Worlds.

Who would believe the great Orson would one day cavort with their little son John in exotic Colonial Hong Kong?

* * *

A short walk away, renowned artist *Thomas Gainsborough* dominated the Market Hill. I was told he was privileged to paint the portraits of some of the great 18th Century founders of the British Empire. My young eyes riveted on his frightening image and I gripped my mother's hand in awe.

The town's famous painter stood way above on his pedestal in bronzed splendour, gazing spectrally out over the market in the bustling little eastern English town of Sudbury. Two hundred years before, little Tommy also held onto his mother's hand in that same busy local farmers' marketplace which had survived since the Middle Ages.

The war dragged on and the air raid sirens would suddenly blare, quickly emptying the market and sending us scuttling to public shelters, abandoning Thomas.

The Very Reverend Cannon Hughes

This self-important Church celebrity, the redoubtable, balding *Reverend Cannon Hughes* had an ethereal, superior high-voiced Welsh accent, which none of us locals from Suffolk understood. The parishioners were far too polite to mention it, but the entire parish spent two decades having no clue what he was talking about. But he had been sent to us by God, or at least by the Bishop from Bury St Edmond's Cathedral.

He obviously considered himself intellectually superior to his flock and emphasised his status by always wearing a dog collar and smart black suits, identifying himself as a gentleman in our informal farming town.

Different scares awaited in nearby St Peter's Church, where Christians had reportedly worshiped since 1180. On Sunday my father's beliefs were celebrated in the local pub, but my mother took me to the sober, spookily massive church. I gazed up in awe at *The Lord Jesus*, high above. He was almost naked, very white and scary, with His realistic body hanging, bleeding on a wooden cross above the altar. Fortunately, His eyes were closed.

They said He would return to claim His own Empire. Meanwhile we would manage ours on His behalf and I would be educated as a working-class clerk for the Empire.

* * *

The ancient stone church, de-steepled in the war effort, is treasured for its coloured cut-glass windows, a heritage from the weaving industries and prosperous post-mediaeval times. There, the Saviour was illustrated in the windows, in His better times as the loving shepherd of His flock, a tall, graceful young man with groomed blond hair, clad in shimmering robes. He held little lambs, and His bright shining blue eyes bore directly into mine, probing and questioning.

He was the Son of a similar fatherly white male God, somewhere up there, sent from Heaven to instruct us in converting and guiding the Heathen throughout the Empire.

He helped me to deal with my terrible childhood sins. I spoke to Him regularly, in tightly closed-eyed prayer, but fortunately He never spoke back.

Resplendent in my red cassock and brilliant white surplice, my piping voice attempted in vain to compete with the thundering pipe organ pounded by the show-off Mr Nicholson.

At the Rectory Bible lessons we had no idea what the Welsh Man of God was talking about. But we got tea and biscuits. By the time I left the liberal Grammar School, however, I was totally disillusioned.

* * *

Sex was not represented at all as a sin in our mild brand of the Anglican religion which thankfully packed churches on Sundays and festival occasions. The Cannon's thundering Welsh sermons, however, apparently advised about pride, envy, wrath, sloth, greed and gluttony.

My two older sisters gleefully told me about *lust*, a puzzle at that stage.

The subject of sex was discussed occasionally but very openly around our happy family table as an enjoyable human activity; also, I learned, useful for propagation.

My attractive elder sister was fair game for the randy soldiers and airmen from overseas crowding our little town and who could die on raids over Germany the next day. All their local English male competition had gone off to war to save the Empire.

This was long before 'the Pill', so pregnancy was a concern for the lusty girls whose airmen lover could just literally fly off in the night, never to return. Our young women supported the war effort with gusto! Discarded condoms were common behind the pubs and the village dance halls. We kids blew them up to wave for patriotism and scandalise the local old ladies.

The Americans also came armed with silk stockings and Camel cigarettes, all very strong bargaining tools.

My sister Bubbles, was doing her part for the war effort, working in a listed factory which produced radiators and parts for the essential lorries, as we called them.

She was in her late teens when the Royal Air Force and the Yanks opened their fully operational, day and night airfields (of course we called them aerodromes!) flooding the town with lonely young men.

Competing parties, dances and essentially any lure was employed by the airbases to attract them, and the girls and townsfolk reciprocated at Town Hall hops, in the pubs and by home invitation.

Life at war could be short; certainly everyone's time was limited. Thus, it was party time, and frantic swing, jive or jitterbug were the dances. My sisters spent their spare time disrupting our small household, practising their latest dancing moves from scratchy thick phonograph records.

England had its staid Harry Roy Orchestra, but onto the scene came an American dance band icon: *Glenn Miller*! He arrived as a highly publicised Major in the US Army, but with his also uniformed full orchestra in tow. They transfixed London, the Allied Forces and the essential communicator, the BBC. Soon everybody, including a young country lad like me, were humming *In The Mood*, *Moonlight Serenade* or *Chattanooga Choo-Choo*.

Glenn Miller and his show music had invaded my life, but alas all too briefly.

Major Miller had a band tour arranged 'at the front line', for Allied troops actively fighting in France during the invasion. In that cold December in 1944, he took off in a small plane to cross the English Channel to join the band, but he never arrived.

Many reports, books and even movies have been made about this drama, but there was never any trace of his plane, and it is just assumed that for some reason it crashed and disintegrated in the sea.

My sister, at the end of the war, did marry *Joe Brown*, an RAF flier from one of those bases, but he actually and successfully preferred The Smooch!

* * *

As the war dragged on, after long days in the family business, Sunday afternoon was my parents' uninterrupted time in bed together. For us it was Sunday School with Cannon Hughes droning on and on and on.

My little singing voice matured and I became the head boy chorister even recording with His Master's Voice on Oxford Street in battened-down, bombed London, *Oh, For The Wings Of A Dove* and *Hear My Prayer*.

* * *

How easily are some celebrities forgotten! Half a century later my young grandchildren were puzzled when I ask them the significance of Easter. "Tell me about Jesus," I asked. "Is that an Easter bunny?" one of them asked hopefully.

Jesus may not have made it out of the little Sudbury, but Gainsborough did. So would I!

* * *

My admittedly reasonably well-to-do great-grandfather had shares in the local flour mill, several businesses and had been a Sudbury Council alderman.

He luxuriously installed a bathroom at the height of fashion, when the eponymous *Thomas Crapper* opened the first-ever sink, bath and flushing toilet bathroom business in London in 1880.

So, as a family we were not totally deprived, and as we grew older, we used the bath in my grandfather's large old family house, within walking distance.

Most townfolk around us had very basic facilities, some still even had water wells and squeaky hand pumps. Indoor plumbing and frills only became widespread when the socially minded Labour Party offered popular upgrading financial assistance after the war.

From the age of six we all walked across the town to school with our gas mask bouncing on our side in its cardboard box. At school, fearing German poisoned-gas bomb attacks, we struggled to breathe, practising in the tight-fitting rubber contraptions. Then on the way home we lined up at the railway station in relief to throw stones at the arriving miserable little Cockney kids being evacuated from the heavily bombed London.

The war dragged on for years, then without warning our little town was packed with convoys of allied soldiers heading to the coast for the invasion of Europe. Enemy aircraft overhead were silenced, but the fighting in Europe and 'over there' continued for a couple of years.

And in just those few years my young mind had absorbed Pearl Harbor, the aerial Battle of Britain, the Blitz of London and bombing of South England, which I experienced. As I matured I followed the warship and freighter battle of the Atlantic and the glamorous North Africa desert campaign.

Then the battles moved up Italy and finally the invasion of Europe led to Germany itself.

I was old enough to comprehend the salacious details of the fate that befell *Il Duce Mussolini* and his consort *Claretta Petacci* on April 28, 1945, near Milan.

He was caught with his pretty young mistress, while his wife and family sensibly stayed safely back at home. Claretta had just not selected the right boyfriend! After she and Benito were shot by partisans who captured them by chance, they were strung up by their feet in public and ridiculed.

Adolf Hitler must have been poor company for his longtime girlfriend *Eva Braun* down in the Berlin *Fuhrenbunker* in those final days, and it had looked as though the Russians were going to get them first. They solved the problem by sensibly committing suicide two days later on April 30, 1945, and were immediately cremated.

The news of Hitler's death was celebrated wildly in the pubs of our little town, as was the immediate official ending of European hostilities on VE-Day, May 8. In fact it became one continuous celebration with street parties and bunting.

The absolute ending of the World War came by using atomic weapons in Japan finalising things on VJ-Day August 15, 1946.

And that was that!

Except that my third wartime celebrity villain, *General Franco*, carried on unscathed and unchallenged, controlling the Spain he seized by untold violence. He lived a long life of luxury and in 1975 died, untroubled in bed, still the surviving Dictator.

The war was over, it was 1946, and the remaining Empire was saved for the moment. My wooden Tommy-gun had long been retired. But times were changing.

Headmaster Gillingham

By the time I was readying for high school at the end of the War in 1947, India and Pakistan rowdily became difficult, then completely independent, although practical enough to remain in the expanding Commonwealth. The Commonwealth ministers all agreed republics and countries could join their club and the modern money-based organisation was created.

This had started a general exodus and they were quickly followed into independence by Jordan, Israel, Ceylon, Libya and Burma. Nevertheless, at the end of the War, we in England were grateful to the Empire, or Commonwealth or whatever it was now called officially, for rallying to save the Old Country.

But to us there was still the existing Empire, and I was going to the Grammar School in preparation for its service.

* * *

How had the relatively small British Isles developed our powerful Empire?

The country itself was accustomed to these annoying attacks but their great strength and reason for their survival was simply that they occupied a defensible island. It had worked again.

At school we had learned that many hundreds of years before, the east coast of England had been continuously swarmed by Angles, Saxons, Jutes and adventurous Germanic tribes from the continent who undertook the dangerous trip across the Channel from the mainland. Then much more skillful sailors, the Danes and

Norse Vikings, plundered us, philandering on our east coast and the northern areas, leaving evidence of their invasions with blue eyes and blond hair.

Then came the more highly cultured Romans, raising our standards for 300 years until their Empire too failed; followed by the infamous Normans in 1066. We learned and watched as the Normans also set out to conquer Wales, but it would still take a couple of hundred years for the wild northern Welsh fellows to join. The Scots are still uncertain.

In 1171 the somewhat united island set out merrily to plunder our very own, first overseas colony: Ireland.

This all sounds very grand, but to put it into perspective, when the Normans came, London was a small town accessible by the Thames River and the total population in the entire country was only about two and a half million people, which just grew slowly during the next 500 years.

It was only after 1500 the population started expanding sharply and exceeded five million by the mid-sixteen hundreds. The first modern census of the entire country in 1801 recorded ten and a half million people; now it is about 68 million.

While we were playing around locally, obsessed with our island, the Europeans had sailed away and discovered North America for themselves in the famous 1492, and started conquering, occupying and taking over other, often exotic lands, which became the accepted thing to do. England joined in enthusiastically and we went on cheerfully expanded our acquisitions by force for some 400 years.

The Reverend Hughes assured us we were bringing Christ to the native world, so it was all good.

Our problems had started when our successful, strong territories began making trouble, intent upon their own independence. Losing the United States in 1776 had been bad enough, but Canada had not helped, going off on their own way in 1867.

In the new century first Australia, then New Zealand, South Africa, Afghanistan, Egypt and Iraq had pulled away.

As I grew more sophisticated, I was to learn that our resolve had been further eroded with the Balfour Declaration in 1926 when British

Empire communities were unbelievably 'to be equal in status, in no way subordinate to each other, united in common allegiance to the Crown and freely associated members of the British Commonwealth of Nations'.

This had been made even worse by the Statute of Westminster, when the British Government said it would 'not enact a law unless a Dominion government had expressly requested or agreed to it'.

Which all brought me to a high school education in a quickly diminishing Empire.

* * *

"Three on each hand and you know the drill; pull away and you get double."

The skinny, tall, skeletal, old fellow whacked as hard as he could, his eyes squeezed almost shut in his masochistic frenzy, spital flying from his mouth. I knew I would not be able to use my hands again for a few days, but it was quickly over.

Those canings came later, and at the beginning, just after the war had ended, the legendary, gaunt old *Headmaster Gillingham* was always in stiff collar and tie, his black suits hanging from his lank spectral form. He never smiled and viewed the entire world through squinting, suspicious eyes. However, he was all forced welcoming grimaces as he made our acquaintance in the high school first form.

The all-male, uniformed Grammar School, founded by *William Woods* in 1491, had a high standard of education, producing a steady stream of scholars for the nearby Cambridge University. It was steeped in formality, tradition and discipline, designed to prepare men to serve their country and Empire!

I vividly remember my practical first form teacher saying we were not there for an education. "You are here to pass the School Leaving Certificate, your passport out of this slum, and then to serve your country!" he instructed cynically.

Then he ordered that we open our Empire apologist Rudyard Kipling! *"If you keep your wits about you while all others are losing theirs and blaming you … you'll be a man, my son."*

The rule was strict discipline. Stand when the teacher enters. Keep quiet unless addressed. Call all the students by their surnames; I was simply Death. We were pushed to excel in a very competitive system and failures were ridiculed and punished. Misbehavior brought detention or canning.

I was proud and elated to be there!

* * *

My early mentor was the bullying sports master, Elly Ellison. I was a robust competitive lad and jumped to his command. He marked me first in the gymnasium class for my entire school career. I excelled in athletics and was progressively awarded the various sports teams colours.

Although several years younger than the senior boys, I doggedly got up an hour early every day for six weeks before the Open School cross-country race, to run the entire course. By the time of the race, I knew every step of the way, sprinted confidently to the front and never saw another runner.

On sports day I entered every event available to me, middle and senior school, competing continuously the entire afternoon and personally winning enough points for my house to claim the shield. The final event was the celebrated mile I expected to win, but, exhausted, only dragged myself to third place.

Several of our teachers were back from the war and turned out in uniform on parade with the School Cadet Corps. Elly went even further by appointing me Drum Major of the school band allowing me to strut around in a fancy uniform like a peacock. I was becoming precocious beyond belief but ideal material for the Empire.

* * *

However, my scholastic activities were erratic, either extremely high or abject failures depending upon my attitude to the teacher. I literally hated my Latin teacher, *Tishy.*

He was a nasty little man given to approaching suddenly from the rear and striking students over the knuckles with his heavy metal-tipped ruler. He got his comeuppance, when a student called McQuhae, grown bigger than he was, finally rebelled at being knuckled and felled him with one punch.

Tishy was left lying between the rows of desks as we all stared in hope at his still form. "You've killed him, McQuhae," we cheered. But to our regret Tishy moved! The boy's father was a wealthy school governor known to provide hefty donations and popular McQuhae, after a severe caning of course, was soon back in the class but with Tishy's bullying, knuckling days over.

Not so the feared *Headmaster Gillingham*, the publicly respected, revered celebrity at the Headmaster's Conference.

* * *

Having worked for a couple of hours in the family business that morning as usual, I was late for assembly. I was met by Head Boy Neil Salmon. A teachers' pet, Salmon had set up a little desk at the door to the gym to book late-comers.

Usually, you could just slip in quietly at the back, but Salmon smirked triumphantly. "You are late, Death. That is a detention."

"You ran down the corridor," he added, "that's another one." And, he laughed, "You didn't keep to the left side, so that's a third detention."

The highly completive houses competed for the coveted shield. Salmon was in another house and this was high politics at play because three detentions meant missing sports. A big game was at stake, so naturally I punched the much older Salmon hard in the face, as he deserved.

In morning assembly, the school sang classic, patriotic and inspiring anthems between prayers,

"Bring me my bow of burning gold,
bring me arrows of desire,
bring me my spear; O clouds unfold,
bring me my chariots of fire!"

Outside, Salmon fell to the floor, blood pouring down the front of his crisp white shirt, screaming demonstratively in pain. The assembly inside disrupted in confusion. Mr Gillingham appeared in a fury! "Go to my study, boy," he shouted at me.

* * *

My long wait was the worst part but eventually I heard his loud, "Come!"

No discussion, just the expected "Choose a stick, boy!"

I contemplated the usual choices in his infamous stick stand and chose a stout ash, with minimum flexibility. I was too big to be bent over his desk, as had happened previously, so this would be on my hands.

Back in the class I was a hero, of course, and had triumphed for my house. A caning over-rode detentions and I would be free to play for Jamison House in the next all-important game.

This was the necessary corporal punishment that had built the stiff upper lip of the British Empire! Take it like a man. It was a demonstration of the decisive violent action upon which the Empire was founded and my first lesson in practical politics.

Brigadier General Walter Stirling

My great war hero, fighting to protect our overseas possessions, was *Lt Colonel David Stirling, 'The Fantom'*, who had been labelled as 'quite mad'. He had been thrown out of nearby Cambridge University for carousing and eventually ended up serving in the Guards in the North African desert, founding the new Special Air Services unit, SAS. They parachuted or drove behind enemy lines carrying out highly dangerous, but critically devastating raids. He caused havoc to the enemy, attacking within their territory, despite appalling losses.

He was finally captured, tried several daring escapes, and ended up in Colditz, Germany's most secure prison. I idolised him and could not believe it when I learned my Boy Scouts mentor and returned military hero, *Brigadier General Walter Stirling*, was his uncle. I listen spellbound to Brig's tales of his nephew's glory!

It was appropriate just after the war that the initial celebrities to mentor me were military. The County Boy Scout Commissioner, Walter Stirling, 'Brig', as we all called him, emerged as my next influencer. The general was a tall, kindly man often appearing in full scouting uniform, complete with kilt or shorts and exposed knobby knees. He was famously married to an Austrian princess and lived in a vast country estate which we Scouts enjoyed for camping and other activities, in which he joined wholeheartedly.

Boy Scouts was founded as an international youth activity by the militarian, *Lord Baden Powell* following the Boer War and still attracting prominent soldiers who enjoyed instructing young boys.

Chief Scout Lord Rowallen

I became obsessed earning badges, was elevated as a top-ranking King Scout and grandly travelling to London to allow the Chief Scout, *Lord Rowallen,* (another famous military man) to have a full day in my presence. The Lord always wore full scouting uniform including his kilt when he was with me and played the role of Chief Scout seriously in a superior, detached establishment way. He may have been a Scout, but he was always the general!

I represent the United Kingdom at the 1951 World Scout Jamboree in Austria, my first trip abroad, providing the kilted Lord Rowallen with a second time in my company.

But then my elevated teenage ego and my world collapsed!

***

In my teens we had grandly moved into the big old family home, my status vastly improved. It was half-timbered, hundreds of years old and boasting an enormous wood log fireplace, where we hosted still genuinely Dickensian gatherings!

However, the generations' old family bakery business had run into problems due to a national flour-milling monopoly and factory-produced 'sliced bread'. After long family debate, I left the Grammar School early and went to work full-time, supporting myself financially.

My father was educated more by the First World War, trained to drop bombs by hand over the side of his Sopwith Camel biplane, naturally on Germans. However, the war ended before he had that pleasure.

I had just turned sixteen, admittedly a progression over my grandfather who left the lowly Mill Street school at twelve and my father at fourteen. But I had an objective!

In the summer of 1952, the highly respected Imperialist, *King George the Fifth* died, and the young *Princess Elizabeth* returned dramatically from a trip to our Kenya colony with her husband *Prince Philip*. He now respectfully walked several steps behind our future Queen. I mourned my War-time King in Bury St Edmond's Cathedral.

Thirty-five years later, I was halfway around the world chatting self-consciously with Prince Philip, while a couple of burly security guys breathed down my neck.

Union Chair Mr Carter

I was leaving grade school and very aware of a celebrity politician called *Attlee.* My folks disparagingly called him 'a socialist' but *The Honorable Clement Attlee* was Prime Minister of Great Britain from 1945 to 1951.

"The Left was never Right!" my father stormed.

Clement Attlee was obviously popular to many, however. The war had sent the men to fight and their women to manufacture, and they all started unhelpfully to demand higher pay and more of the take, just at the wrong time, when Empire's revenues were failing. Hence the old warrior Churchill was dumped and the avowed socialist Attlee was comfortably elected.

The non-colonising countries, particularly Germany and Italy, which had mostly missed out originally on the colonial spoils, had wrecked everything by starting the two world wars and now the US and the USSR were taking over. Losing control, the British steep decline had started.

While upper middle class, an Oxford graduate and a barrister, Attlee had converted to social work and teaching before joining parliament in 1922.

He had a brilliant career, serving in the First World War military, being Deputy Prime Minister during the Second World War and elected as the national leader. He had an extremely socially minded agenda and brought in hundreds of measures intending to change the way the country operated.

While succeeding Conservative governments attempted to reverse things, his measures have changed social policy in the UK and throughout the world. He introduced national insurance and the National Health System in 1948. He financed and built massive public housing projects throughout the country. He maintained full employment, and enlarged social services generally provided by the state and nationalised key services and industries.

He pushed decolonisation and worked to dismantle the oppressive Empire.

Most important from my personal point of view at the time, Clement Attlee introduced national parks and country access, built new towns and had installed the Town and Country Planning ministry to introduce a national land use planning and zoning program.

I was intent upon leaving high school to take part in this noble exercise and barely sixteen, in mid-1951, I enrolled as a full-time trainee with the Suffolk County Council's new Planning Department in the nearby Bury St Edmund's.

The recent science and profession of City Planning had been launched. In a friendly office atmosphere, my daily school name softened from Death to John!

* * *

To this point I had almost exclusively been with males and to my acute embarrassment girls came into my life. It was to be several years before I was comfortable in female company.

That was, of course, except for *Shirley.*

There were a few prominent and wealthy families in the Sudbury district who had sent their children to private schools and who spoke with plummy accents. Shirley was attractive, about thirty and flaunted her celebrity, wealth and 'superior' upbringing. She also had a liking for maturing boys which I discovered to my great delight when I was sixteen.

Her family mansion was set in an extensive ornamental garden and my first happy introduction to Shirley's ways was an invitation for a summer lemonade while she pruned her rhododendrons. I found her deep in the bushes, in a tiny bikini; nonchalantly topless.

This developed into an invitation to learn to drive her splendid new car. With me proudly behind the wheel, in quiet English country lanes, she quickly demonstrated her intimate approaches to gearshift and clutch techniques. The 'driving lessons' became an escalating but back lane parked routine and I could not believe my good luck.

But decades later I met a school friend from that time who had enjoyed the same good fortune, and I was devastated when I learned I had missed the advanced lessons in the back seat!

Still, we did not converse very much, so she did not improve my knowledge of fully dressed females or increase my comfort in their company.

* * *

After two years growing up in an office mainly manned by young fellows just returned from the war, I met an essential financial benefactor, *Mr Carter,* a grey-headed, chatty local celebrity. He ran the County Education Department and chaired the branch of the National Association (Union) of Government Employees. He was a fussy, burly little man who always listened quietly and sympathetically. He was loved by all and made a perfect union leader! We worker proletariat met regularly in the cafeteria, plotting rebellion.

Sitting drinking tea, after such a Union meeting, he suddenly said, "You can do better than this, John", and proceeded to get me admitted into college, through work credits and financial support from the county.

In 1952 I was accepted at the College of Estate Management in Kensington, a part of London University, starting an education in real estate and began my social elevation in the overawing big city of London.

Mitford

"*Mitford!*" he introduced himself loudly at dinner in a small Bayswater Hotel in Central London, never offering his first name.

At the time, just after the war, the Mitford name was notorious and books, musicals and movies were later made of their exploits. Mention of Mitford immediately raised *Oswald Mosley* and then *The Mitford Sisters*.

He was a big blustery fellow with an exaggerated Etonian accent and a braying voice used to command attention. Even I had heard of the Mitfords. Here was a social celebrity but attending the same college!

English country towns, like Sudbury, were essentially class free and Mitford's cultivated upper-class voice and arrogance for the first time made me acutely aware of my lower-class Suffolk country upbringing and accent, leaving me mumbling in response.

* * *

At college we never knew our Mitford's actual lineage, although the girls in the office confirmed he was genuine. It seemed he was connected in some way to the *Second Baron, David Mitford, The Right Honourable the Lord Redesdale,* who was an eccentric, prone to wild tantrums. The Lord was unable scholastically to get into Eton or later Sandhurst for a military career, which took a lot of doing for a Lord, and was sent off instead to plant tea in the colonies.

But he served with distinction in the First World War and even adventured at gold mining in Canada near the aptly named Swastika district in Northern Ontario.

Apt, because the Swastika was the Nazi symbol and his wife and some of his daughters induced him to support the rising *Hitler* in Germany. His married daughter Diana was having an affair with the leader of the British Union of Fascists, *Sir Oswald Mosley.* She divorced and wed Mosley, the Baronet of Ancoats, with great publicity, at the home of *Joseph Goebbels* in 1936 in Germany with *Adolf Hitler* as the guest of honour.

David Mitford and his wife attended the notorious Nuremberg Rally in November 1938 in Germany, where they were charmed personally by Adolf. During the War, Mosley and Diana were, of course deservedly, thrown into English jail, hopefully on bread and water!

His daughter Unity Mitford was even more a Nazi fanatic and totally besotted by Hitler, personally telling him she was prophetically conceived in Swastika, Canada. She attempted suicide in Munich the day War was declared and never recovered. She died in 1948 after the Nazi defeat.

Another daughter *Jessica Mitford* perversely became a raving communist and never spoke to them. Only one relatively normal daughter, *Nancy Mitford,* later chronicled the family adventures, and was actively anti-fascist. Just a normal elite, upper-class English family.

David's only son was killed by the war in Burma. Poor David Mitford.

* * *

Next morning in Bayswater, it was raining. My personal celebrity *Mitford* strode into the Bayswater Road waving his umbrella and bellowing "Taxi, taxi!" One screeched to a halt and he threw himself in. I intended to walk to school across the Regent's Park, never having been in a taxi, but it was too late.

Outside the college he nonchalantly threw some cash at the driver and shouted at me, "Your turn tomorrow." The next morning, I got up early and crept out before Mitford was around, not to be caught in a taxi fare embarrassment.

What became of our college friend Mitford? He soon dropped out of lectures citing his demanding social life. It seemed he decided very quickly the lower-class students and serious studies were not for him. But behind the bombast he was a very cheerful, pleasant fellow.

And I must thank him for giving me my first 'putdown' education in the British Class System. I had to make changes!

Stride of Stride House

Mitford moved on, no doubt into an expensive mews cottage in Mayfair; but I to super-exclusive Kensington, thanks totally to Mr Stride. I got on well with him immediately we met, and I spent hours in future years drinking tea in his suite and hearing his adventures in the Empire countries.

Stride House was a large, terraced residence, providing suites of impossibly expensive student accommodation for the very wealthy. It was in stylish Kensington a walking distance from my college. My unit was perfect, and I lived there very happily for the next few years, right in the centre of London.

Mr Stride was a big name in the student housing community proudly telling his tales of taking advantage of his government position to accumulate enough 'loot' as he called it to become a renowned central London property owner!

He rented every available square foot and had converted a broom closet under the grand sweeping staircase into a tiny one-space unit by punching a window in the wall looking out into the central 'light' well, which accommodated all the plumbing and services.

There was a bed, a curtained hanging closet for my few clothes and a hand basin with a fold-down table above it for studying, while sitting at the end of the bed. A shared bathroom was just down the hall and Mrs Stride cleaned and provided tea and toast every morning.

Absolutely perfect! I now nonchalantly (often) mentioned that I had "an apartment in Kensington".

* * *

In 1953 there was an enormous London street party, to celebrate the coronation of *Queen Elizabeth.* Pubs were overflowing and the surging crowds vied for positions on the parade route.

Somewhere in that happy hoard with me was South African Tokkie Smith, who was later to become my close friend in the Crown Colony of Hong Kong and one of the celebrated names in rugby history.

* * *

Those carefree years went by quickly, and eventually we students completed our studies. I spent six weeks before the final exams shut in my room feverishly studying and won a national academic prize, which was to change my life.

As college ended, however, I sat, desolate, in the library without a job. I had the top marks, so my pals jubilantly laughed at my plight. "Who wants to hire anyone called Death from a lowly Grammar School?" they chortled correctly from their privileged private school status. "Even if he does have an apartment in Kensington."

Death is a common family name in farming East Anglia and considered distinctive. It came with Flemish weavers from the little town of Ath who had resettled across the Channel in the Eastern counties. Hence d'Ath, then anglicised to Death.

My fellow students thought it hilarious to come up with optional spellings to use on my next job applications, d'Ath (their favourite), D'Ath, D'Eath, d'Eath, etc. A real estate company in the trendy West End called Cullens immediately accepted me as *John D'Eath,* the name on the application, which then became my new improved identity by deed poll.

I had learned that to succeed in the Empire, one must at least appear to be somewhat upper-class in this class-controlled society. My accepted image by an establishment company in Hong Kong was later to prove this point.

* * *

But before that could happen, I had National Service. Military action was still essential to control denizens of the waning Empire and of necessity the United Kingdom retained compulsory service, requiring a couple of years of army training for all young men.

It was compulsory for all males at age eighteen but like all students I successfully used educational excuses to defer my entry. I strung it out until 1957. This was just as well, because I would have landed in the middle of the Empire's final military hurrah – the 1956 Suez Canal Crisis in Egypt.

* * *

By the time I left grade school the real world was already back in turmoil. Russia had closed its borders and America was sinking into its Red Funk seeing a Communist under every bed. Civil war was raging in Korea.

Emerging out of all that chaos came another of my heroes from the War, General Eisenhower, 'Ike'.

His image was everywhere during the war as *General Dwight D.*

Eisenhower, Supreme Commander of the Allied Expeditionary Force in Europe.

He had just returned into the European news becoming the first commander of the new NATO military force in 1951.

My personal concern was to avoid the Korean War which had divided the Korean peninsula between fiercely waring armies into which the British Army had plunged.

I did not wish to take part, but I could see compulsory military service looming. It could be held at bay as long as I could justify continued study, so I determined to become a perpetual student.

The Battle of Imgin River had claimed over six hundred British military lives in one horrendous battle and strengthened my resolve!

A couple of years later in January 1953, Ike had given up on that minor job and had become President of the United States.

A curious tale about that period emerged in my life, fifty years later. One of my business partners in Santa Monica, a prominent property owner, had served his time in the American Air Force in their atomic weapon division. His name was *Edward Ellis.*

His account was that early in 1953 his crew had transported an atomic device to an American air base in Japan, preparatory to potential use in the Korean War.

The war was ended by Eisenhower and Kim Il Sung in July later that year, but there are many rumours Ike threatened him with use of a nuclear weapon intervention.

Ed was convinced his load was real and everything was handled, he said, "with the utmost damned respect". But who knows? It did not need to be armed for the bluff to work. Or was the General war crazy and serious?

For whatever reason, my personal concern about going to Korea was solved by the armistice and a land deal, but replaced with other Empire concerns like the uncooperative Egypt Suez Canal, Mau Mau in Kenya, Malayan communist insurgents, unrest in the Aden hills and so on.

These were enough to keep me alarmed and studying hard.

* * *

The Egyptian resistance forces waged several years of effective bloody activity against the continuing British occupation following the Second World War, which saw extensive battles in North Africa.

This came to a fighting conclusion over the brief period of October and November 1956 causing the British and French to back down and leave the country. They claimed, disparagingly, the Egyptians would never be competent enough to manage the Suez Canal on their own!

The 'allies' had not been backed by the United States and this was a critical signal that the decolonisation of the Middle East, Africa and the world was underway.

During that period in 1956 the last of the British troops were forced out of Egypt. With a sigh of relief, I then consented to begin my military training and reluctantly had a final cup of tea with Mr Stride and gave up my apartment in Kensington.

* * *

Our fierce, moustache-spiked, regimental sergeant was there to shock us into being soldiers. "Hands off cocks and pull-on socks," he screamed at 6am, banging the barracks garbage bin with his swagger-stick.

He warned us the natives had been acting up in Egypt again and the military was on alert throughout the Empire. Now I was really creeping through the woods training and carrying a real machine gun.

"Come under fire; drop; roll to cover; observe; return fire." The problem was they discovered a weakness in my right eye. On the firing range I apparently sprayed bullets wildly and was summarily discharged from the Army!

They seemed happy to be rid of me and I had no interest in staying anyway unless I could become an upwardly mobile officer!

* * *

I had captained the college soccer team and played for the London University Sidonians. But I also joined Woodford Rugby Club to switch from the working-class football and improve my social standing by playing rugger!

The old, true joke in England is that football (soccer) is a gentlemen's game played by hooligans. But that rugby is a hooligan's game played by gentlemen.

I finished out my Army days just playing rugby at Aldershot.

Colonisation

The Empire was clearly under pressure although it still held a significant number of countries under its control. Emerging nations were flexing their muscles.

After the war, while I was at high school, significant countries, India, (later partly Pakistan), Jordan, Israel, Myanmar and Sri Lanka pulled out and took their independence.

This was a big hole in our previously controlled world. These were countries which emotionally inspired so many Victorians with romantic accounts of our valiant British Empire builders.

Then, during my college and army experience Libya, Sudan, Ghana and Malaya had left. What was happening to my Empire? I was about to find out.

Taipan Sir John Keswick

The old Empire's money-making attitude towards 'drug dealers' had changed publicly since the17th century, when its official support produced damaging effects upon China sufficient to cause the first Opium Wars from 1839 to1842.

In 1832 Scottish partners William Jardine and James Matheson had set out to trade in Asia, their main commodity becoming opium, supported by cotton, tea and silk. They operated perfectly legally from the British Empire in India, which produced the drug and initially settled upon Canton as their distributing base in China.

In 1842 they set up their main business centre in the new Crown Colony of Hong Kong and consolidated their trade with the help of

British naval and military power by way of the highly successful (for them!) Opium Wars with China.

When I discovered Jardine in January 1958, they were still apparently operating highly successfully in Hong Kong. It was, for me, to be a rags-to-riches discovery!

* * *

Now demobbed from military service, I was totally broke and looking desperately for work. The fellows at the Chartered Surveyors Institute knew me because I had won their Institutional Prize and recommended me to a 'Jardine Matheson', of which I had never heard. They advised me to attend an interview with a chap called Sir John Keswick.

As usual when I had no money my kind Winchester sister Bubbles had taken me in. Public library research revealed Jardines as the leading British trader in the Orient, suggested coyly they originated as successful opium drug dealers. That looked a profitable start, I thought. Now they were a massive general trading company also controlling Hong Kong's largest real estate company.

I read newspaper reports about the increasing independence negotiations we were having with our seventy or so remaining Empire countries around the world.

Tiny Hong Kong had, however, missed my notice.

In the government's mysterious Whitehall, the massive switch was underway, replacing the outdated Empire with a British Commonwealth of Nations.

Back in the previous century a very short-term, trouble-making Prime Minister, Lord Rosebery had talked about giving nations 'independence within a commonwealth of nations'. The title and idea had stuck.

I knew my hero Winston Churchill had taken the issue a big step further during the war in 1944, calling a 'Commonwealth Prime Ministers Conference' with Mackenzie King, Jan Smuts, Peter Fraser and John Curtin representing Canada, South Africa, New Zealand and Australia.

Then, after the war, The Commonwealth of Nations was formalised in London and the British Empire was, of necessity, being dismantled, although I sadly noted they had dropped the word British from the Commonwealth title. But where did Hong Kong fit into all this? Should I consider leaving safe England?

* * *

The most newsworthy current Keswick, I learned, was *Sir William 'Tony' Keswick.* He had a remarkable career in the Empire capped by surviving a murder attempt on him by the Japanese in Shanghai. Then he went on to head the British Secret Service in the Pacific War.

Now he was a director of the mighty Bank of England.

Challenged in the equally powerful High Court with alleged insider trading, he had recently displayed his confidence and social status when he had been asked by the judge whether he was indeed playing golf when the alleged deed had occurred. He replied confidently, "No, your honour, playing *at* golf." Well, this Jardine had a sense of humour!

I was, however, met by his younger, also distinguished brother *Sir John Keswick*, the Jardine Chairman, in the City of London.

Jardine's office reeked of tradition and prestige, but I saw no sign of drugs. John Keswick was a warm personable gentleman, not a bit like a drug-dealer, who sat me down with a cup of tea and biscuits, making me very comfortable. He was tallish and well-built and smiled his friendly welcome from a full face, below thinning cropped graying hair. His entire attitude was practical and down to earth with no sign of 'side'.

He chatted about the company and his own adventures in Hong Kong and China. I did not really know quite where Hong Kong was, but it all sounded exotic.

He enquired about my life, education and business background. Three things were paramount, I believe. I would not have been invited at all if my name were still Death! D'Eath was much more impressive! Second, rugby was important. Then, my national prize in real estate mainly clinched the deal.

Sir John laughed uproariously that I had just come from military service totally broke, borrowing ten shillings from my sister to take the train to London for him to meet me. That seemed to be the turning point and he said I was hired.

I walked out of the Jardine office onto the familiar crisp English winter sidewalk in a daze.

I still knew nothing about Hong Kong or China, just vaguely where they were. If I had known the mess China was in, I might well have thought twice.

Research then required laborious visits to libraries to consult references and encyclopedias. This was in the early part of 1958. I had learned that Mao Tse-tung had started Communism in China long ago in 1921, taking his party to power in 1949 by revolution after the Sino Chinese war.

But he had recently thrown everything into chaos with his industrial Great Leap Forward which had been having the opposite effect. I was not to know that China was already, as a result, heading fast into the world's largest famine from 1959 to 1961, when some 30 million people were to starve to death. By the time I arrived in Hong Kong China had cut off all connection with the outside world and starving refugees were flooding across the border.

* * *

Amazingly, just a few weeks after my interview, in February 1958, I was on a train again but to Italy, to pick up a first-class Italian cruise liner to Hong Kong. This transformed my life. I sailed rather than flew at Sir John's insistence. "Get the feel of the Middle East and Asia. Explore the old Empire along the way."

John Keswick had also smilingly made me an immediate generous cash advance, and sent me to his tailor, Silvers, in the City of London to be outfitted with a white dinner jacket and tropical clothes for the trip. I discovered that when a tailor asks a gentleman, "How do you dress, sir?" the answer is either "Left" or "Right," to ensure perfect trouser comfort.

* * *

By the Suez Canal I had dined at the Captain's Table. I become proficient at tying my new black bow tie, accustomed to nonchalantly throwing laundry into a basket and to putting my shoes outside the door to be polished by some unseen minion. I was met and entertained by a company contact in Cairo and at each exotic port along the way.

A book from the ship's library, 'How to treat the natives', stressed that etiquette required never to acknowledge their existence and certainly not enter conversation. This particularly applied to table service, the author advised, where they must be pointedly ignored. "They also serve who only stand and wait," she misused Milton humorlessly.

With my carefully concealed working-class background, I perversely decided to do absolutely the opposite. Thereafter, I would smile and acknowledge everyone, celebrity or not! My life in affluence had begun, but I was determined to continue treating people as people.

Still, I was learning that the whole point of being in the 1 per cent was not having to mix with the 99 per cent, unless you choose. This certainly applied to the upper- and lower-deck discrimination on my voyage, and I was beginning to feel suitably superior!

* * *

Nowhere could have been initially more exotic than Egypt and Cairo! Museums, the pyramids, camels, endless deserts, new smells, streets packed with noisy Middle-Eastern people.

I had left the ship at Alexandria, to wind its way through the Suez Canal and had taken a trip into the Cairo with my new friend and fellow traveller, *Arnand,* a young Belgian army officer seconded to the United Nations.

So here I was, finally in rebellious Cairo, where I could easily have been conscripted to fight for the British Army against the Egyptians just 18 months previously. No one mentioned it or appeared to carry any grudges.

We stayed grandly together in a suite at the famous, still very British-styled Shepheard Hotel. Although Egypt had left the Empire in 1922 there was still considerable colonial influence evident.

Fascinated, I wandered the teeming streets alone late at night and let myself quietly into our dark hotel suite. The bedside light clicked on and there was Arnand pointing his pistol at me! Apparently, he was licensed to carry one internationally. No kidding: it is a frightening experience. It was all straight out of Agatha Christie! And believe me you do shake!

We caught up with the ship at Suez and continued through the Arabian Sea to the barren British desert territory of Aden: my first real-life colony! I strolled around trying to appear confident in my new superior status.

* * *

Later, the port of Karachi provided trips into a chaotic, filthy Pakistan, but then further down the coast the sweeping mysterious, misty Bombay, and a first stay at the magnificent Colonial Taj Hotel at the Gateway to India, preserving traditional visions of the grandeur of the Empire.

We sailed on down the west coast of India to Ceylon (now Sri Lanka) for a couple of nights at the cool and gracious Mount Vernon Hotel, a centre of their tea industry. Yet another retired colony, Ceylon had also been finding its way since relatively early independence in 1948. For good reason it has been considered the original Garden of Eden.

* * *

That left docking at the still very British Singapore, obviously with required visits to The Cricket Club and The Long Bar at Raffles Hotel for their unique Singapore Sling. I learned that throughout the Empire, the gentlemen's games were cricket and rugby. Cricket grounds and clubs were located right in the centre of urban areas and were an essential part of privileged colonial life.

I had accommodation provided for me at the smart and very superior, Tanglin Club, which was to be the scene of many happy times in future years.

Although still under British 'emergency rule' protection, Singapore was locally managed, and a troublemaker called *Lee Kuan Yew* was already prominent in the city. He was to reign as their Prime Minister from the following year, 1959 to 1990, but his country first struggled as a part of Malaysia until they achieved complete freedom as Singapore in 1967.

* * *

Now there I was in the South China Sea. Frankly, I was still carried away with the euphoria of the Empire and I was not personally aware of the dramatic changes that were happening and what I was heading into.

It had been inevitable, one day, that major conflict would result from colonisation, wealth grabs and expanding empires.

At home, as long as England had maintained a repressed working class providing cheap labour, their system operated well. They had to be adequately fed, clothed and provided with sports, music halls and plenty of cheap beer and gin. Then the ruling class had men for their estates, armies and later for the coal mines feeding steam engines and their factories.

My experiences in London had drawn me to the suspicion that our revered democracy was only for the wealthy and really a plutocracy. But I was joining them, wasn't I?

As our British territorial aspirations had grown, following the successful example of the warmer-blooded Europeans, our monopolisation of markets expanded, plus our naval and military might, which was needed to dominate and plunder countries at will.

I felt completely safe protected by our mighty British Navy!

Remarkably, we had been led and controlled, and still were, by a surprisingly small number of notables, we might these days politely call Celebrities.

At the height of the British Empire, towards the end of the 19th century, Britain controlled a quarter of the earth's surface and approximately the same percentage of population.

Then, the first half of the 20th century had seen Britain desperately weakened by the First World War and the very evident progressive loss of territories and trade monopolies.

But no nation could still have been more self-confident than the country of my childhood and I was secure in the knowledge that I was 'British and Best,' just like our products were labelled!

I was not yet aware, but my lifetime would witness the final collapse of the mighty British Empire.

The Communists in China had preyed upon their war-weary masses and taken over there, but were in such chaos it would be two decades yet before they sorted themselves out and at least somewhat fed their growing millions. When I arrived in Hong Kong early in 1958, China and Mao Tse-tung had disappeared.

Sir John Keswick had been right, and I sailed into Hong Kong a fully conditioned, confident young colonial manager.

Arriving in the exciting, bustling Crown Colony, I immediately bought an MG TF1500 sports car, to roar off to join the Rugby and Yacht Clubs; an impossible dream three months previously. My new superior life, being met by the right people, had commenced.

Comprador Au Lum

The British Empire did still exist then, at least in the minds of many of the colonials I was meeting. But I realised things were shrinking fast! Hong Kong remained, but as a relatively insignificant, isolated Crown Colony, coping with the obscure changing political arrangements on the Chinese Mainland, as it always had. This time Communism.

China had isolated itself from the world, with its Great Leap Forward, whatever that was, hidden from view but reportedly underway. The Communist fellow, *Mao Tse-tung*, had been in charge there for more than a decade, but things apparently were not going so well for them.

Refugees had been flowing out of China and the population of Hong Kong had grown to an unprecedented two-and-a-half million people. Many were living in teeming mountainside shanty town slums or hastily built, nasty concrete resettlement buildings.

Far away from the hillside squalor, I awoke in an air-conditioned suite with high ceilings, to the clanging of the trams in the street below, and to the sharp click clack of the workers' wooden clogs before plastic soles brought comparative morning peace to the city.

The world had not yet developed an international tourist industry. Hong Kong was a mysterious, remote destination and certainly not a place to visit casually.

China hardly seemed to exist, a massive, brooding presence just up the Pearl River and over the mountainous horizon. Exotic Macao was an easy boat trip across the delta, and great for a quickie weekend. Canton was a forbidden city.

***

The Land Company owned much of the Central District being founded when an enterprising fellow called Sir Paul Chater had the brilliant idea of digging out the steep hillside and creating a flat harbour area. Jardines had cunningly backed him, later taking the company public but retaining de facto control.

I found myself working for the public company, but with Jardine in dubious hands-on manipulation in their own interest which would now be considered problematic. During my nine years in Hong Kong, however, I discovered that beneath the veneer of British correctness, anything went.

They accommodated me for several years in the central Gloucester Hotel, a luxury property the company owned. This was where the renowned comprador *Au Lum* took me under his wing. He was the one actual running The Gloucester, but in colonial style with a personable English fellow, *Vernon Roberts,* nominally manager. Vernon sat grandly in a big front office, while 'Mr Au' ran things from a back room.

Au Lum jumped up from behind his little modest wooden desk and grabbed my hand warmly in welcome. He was a stocky little fellow, full of energy and always with a very direct eye contact. His Chinese colleagues said that he was a strict disciplinarian but of course I never saw that side of him.

The arrangement suited Au Lum fine. He had every conceivable personal money-making scheme going in the hotel, all conducted in Cantonese which few of us Gweilos could understand or bothered to learn. He had been the manager during the Japanese occupation, which took a great deal of personal skill just to stay alive. He owned a restaurant and cake shops, assorted properties and the massive Sea Palace restaurant in Aberdeen Harbour. He was already a wealthy man.

I first got to know him at his Sea Palace, where he rushed in his power boat to fish me out of the filthy harbour water when I lost a drinking game with new Chinese friends, stripped off in his restaurant bar and jumped into the harbour in payment. The game was run in Cantonese, so Au thought I had been taken advantage of and befriended me.

He and his wife were to remain staunch friends during my time in Hong Kong and interestingly later in Canada.

Au Lum had seriously risked his life during the Japanese occupation to throw food and supplies at night over the Prison of War fences to starving European colleagues, never to be forgotten later.

Most of my new friends were Chinese, but Au Lum became my source of the inside dirt on both Gweilos (white ghosts) and local Chinese personalities about whom I needed to know. He undoubtedly saw me as a valuable person to befriend for the future but whatever his motivation he was a font of local knowledge.

* * *

My life was however essentially colonial. I played rugby at the exclusively Football Club, sailed at the Yacht Club and ate lunch at the downtown Cricket Club. The clubs only admitted white expatriates, of course. The Football Club men's bar went further with the brave sign, 'Dogs and women not allowed'. I never did in fact see a woman in the bar, but a few well-behaved dogs!

In the beginning I was too junior for the ultra-exclusive Hong Kong Club, The Golf Club or The Country Club, but those memberships following in due course.

My standard of living was staggeringly different from the vast number of people around me and I lived in a colonial bubble, which was not oblivious but indifferent. Everything was dominated by self-interest.

My dates were automatically white girls from families within that social circle and in any event my employment contract forbade marriage in the first few years without company permission. It went without saying, this precluded liaison with Asian woman; a friend was dispatched 'back home' immediately upon such a dalliance. Blood was to be kept pure in the British Empire, compared to the Latin races who intermarried.

Life was superficial with endless rounds of cocktail parties and events but little meaningful discussion. It was possible to associate closely with 'friends' there for years and not really know anything about them personally. Even to marry one of them, as I found!

Nevertheless, the Hong Kong population was ninety-eight per cent Chinese and mixed races, and progressively most of my friends automatically became locals although they were often educated in Western countries. Joking, they said they were yellow on the outside and white on the inside. I had become heavily involved with them in local business and charitable organisations which were taking up most of my spare time.

* * *

The corruption and pay-off problems were not confined to the Asian population, and we were aware of it every day. Business entertainment was naturally lavish, as always in Asia, involving women offering tempting liaisons.

Even when still junior I got regular entertainment and gifting approaches by local contractors and businessmen. The Land Company decreed it was cultural and we were directed not to cause loss of face and to accept small gifts. 'Small' improved in size with seniority! At

Christmas this meant a room stacked with gifts and enough expensive booze to last the year.

When tap water became undrinkable, I accepted a contractor's offer of a distilled water bottle and rack. Our home amah phoned in panic to say a truck had arrived. The too generous builder had gone one better and was installing a water filtration and cooling plant.

* * *

Significantly, other than taking lessons and knowing useful day-to-day phrases, I never learned much Cantonese. Everything I did was conducted in English. My assistants Lo Yu Yan and Law Wai Fu were always at my elbow for any translation and all serious negotiations were conducted in English. We British colonials did not join the locals; they had to join us.

My Asian friends of those days, mainly from parts of China, later scattered around the world. Some became extremely successful in other lands, becoming celebrities and enriching my future life.

Orson Welles

The Hong Kong Harbour was still junk-filled and teeming with crime in 1958. Illegal refugees poured in, and the colorful bars were packed with available, willing women. Hong Kong was parochial, isolated from the world, and struggling with a depressed economy.

The Triad was being forced out of China, where the Communists killed any competition and Hong Kong was their haven. Expectedly, crime was rampant.

Almost immediately upon arrival I was given a first personal lesson in harsh Asian reality when I attempted to interfere in Triad business.

I had the job of managing our dozen downtown office buildings. I had three assistants and a staff of many hundreds, but I was 23 and I was in charge!

Lo Yu Yan was my senior assistant, a serious little man intent upon teaching me local customs. In each building The Caretaker was supreme, with likeable young Michael Chung in charge of our latest high-rise complex, Jardine House.

I was warned the buildings were controlled by competing criminal factions. The Cantonese are inveterate gamblers and Lo reported to me that the powerful central district Triad had set up an illegal gambling and money-lending racket in the buildings, but said the totally corrupt local police would not intervene.

Michael was rumoured to be criminally involved in Jardine House and personally in debt to the Triad, which he denied. I ordered them to close it all down. They pleaded that it was impossible and that was not how things were done. But with the certainty of a brash young colonial manager, I insisted upon immediate action.

That night Michael Chung mysteriously went off the roof of Jardine House.

* * *

But onto that real, present-day criminal stage strode a giant of fiction – the famous American, *Orson Welles,* still intent upon dramatising ancient concepts of Chinese buccaneers and junk pirate ships.

He was hailed in Hollywood as a genius with an IQ of 185. The young stage actor's radio drama presentation of H.G. Wells' *War of the Worlds* alien invasion had been taken as real, causing a panic.

Building on this early fame he produced the masterpiece movie *Citizen Kane*, followed by others and then his major Harry Lime portrayal in *The Third Man.*

When I learned he had arrived in Hong Kong to make the movie *Ferry to Hong Kong*, with other well-known international actors, I was excited by an invitation to meet him.

Vernon Roberts, from the Gloucester Hotel, served in the War with a handsome fellow called *Anthony Steel* who turned to acting and married the bombshell, *Anita Ekberg.*

According to Vernon, they entertained him to erotic events with starlets when he was on leave in Europe. Through them and *Sylvia Syms,* the English actress, who was starring in the movie, he had met Orson. Vernon said he was dining with Orson and would introduce me.

I enjoyed dinner alone on the splendid Repulse Bay Hotel terrace overlooking the sea, awaiting my summons. I was in my mid-twenties and this was a big deal! I could see the activity at the colourful bar and waited impatiently.

The signal came from Vernon and I sauntered nonchalantly to the bar for the great man to meet me. The obese Mr Welles was the centre of attention but loudly slurring his words and highly intoxicated.

Vernon shouted his introduction and Orson looked my way and voiced a few words of greeting, but with blurred eyes. He was in his mid-40s and his six foot two and over 300-pound frame dominated the bar. He was, however, visibly overweight, and his unusually shaven face shone with perspiration.

He was clearly accustomed to being the centre of attention and was busy expounding on some subject in a slurred, booming voice. At the time he was considered one of the most prominent movie makers and perhaps the best of his time, so I was bitterly disappointed at our brief encounter.

Totally ignored standing on the fringe, I finished my own drink and shuffled off; mortified.

* * *

Not surprising, the movie was a flop artistically and in the theatres. The bulky Welles, made even larger by his white uniform and way past his prime, captained his ferry back and forth between Hong Kong and Macau having adventures burning junks and defeating fierce, ugly Chinese pirates along the way.

An ageing *Curt Jergens* beats off the pirates to impress the pretty young *Sylvia Syms* and save the day. It was a bit of a laughingstock and did Hong Kong absolutely no good at all. Nor Orson!

On the other hand, the following year saw the filming of the more realistic *The World of Suzie Wong*, which was to be a great international success. Staring *Nancy Kwan*, it dramatically put the genuine Hong Kong on the tourist map.

It portrayed Hong Kong realistically, with teeming hillside slums of refugees, exotic junk-filled harbours, and a vast crime underworld of bars offering colourful women. Conversely it also portrayed the modern Hong Kong with its burgeoning commerce and wealthy colonial lifestyle.

Paul Braga, my well-off Macanese architect friend, owned the ultra-modern, ramped, waterfront house on Deep Water Bay, 'Arrowhead', where some of the scenes were shot. There I watched the action and met the stars. A trim *William Holden* dominated the scene, starring with the vivacious, quietly spoken *Nancy Kwan* and interestingly chatty *Sylvia Syms*, who had redeemed herself by staying around to successfully play another role.

That movie was a big box office hit when released in 1960, and naturally great for Hong Kong, as a tourist destination.

Colonel Hugh Dowbiggin

The colonial of all colonials, *Colonel Hugh Blackwell Dowbiggin* stood out among the many. He had been born in 1884 and nurtured in colonial Ceylon. Not many knew his first name, but everyone just addressed him very respectfully as 'Colonel'.

The Colonel was a caricature of the British imperialist. Dapper, stern-faced, cheroot in one hand and a gin in the other, he was elected President of the Football Club at the age of 77. The club was constantly in a financial crisis and needed an establishment, old stock figure like the Colonel as President.

I had seen him stomping around the Football Club clearly considering himself in charge, ordering around the 'boys', the general term he still used for club attendants whatever their age or years of loyal service

I was to feel the lash of the Colonel's tongue attempting on behalf of the rugby section to have rugby player Bill Leong (an 'apparent' Chinese no less!) admitted as a member. The Colonel would not even discuss the possibility, grew red in the face and just waved me away with his cigar in contempt.

And who was I to oppose him? It appeared he was in practice permanent President of the Football Club, an ex-banker and partner of a large financial firm, with an outstanding military background in the Indian Army, a chancellor of the University, Trustee of the Cathedral, chairman of numerous profitable charitable organisations and most importantly, the Ruling Clerk of the Course at the Royal Hong Kong Jockey Club.

These characters, like the Colonel, ran the Empire.

* * *

The club AGM that followed was a packed affair overflowing the upstairs lounge. Finally Bill Leong's mysteriously stalled membership was noisily shouted onto the agenda and brought to the meeting. The club had voted in principle way back in 1960 to allow open membership but it had never happened.

Somehow Bill's application for membership kept getting lost! Our determined rugby section had taken this very seriously. The notice went out: everyone attends! Tokkie Smith, our popular captain, jumped up and loudly stated he was prepared to resign over the issue.

The diehard colonialist Dowbiggin eventually stormed out, brandishing his walking stick and shouting "I will never allow a Chinese in my club."

Bill Leong was unanimously elected the first ethnic and rugby-playing Chinese member.

Compared to the irascible Colonel, Bill was a charming local oil executive, English educated with a posh accent, and he was a very tough scrum half. He was later a rugby team captain.

The situation was quite ridiculous. Good natured and patient as always, Bill was cheered as he bought his first official round at the packed Men's Bar.

The drama was all behind us when we donned our black ties and Bill and his wife could join us for the annual Football Club dinner dance at the grand old Repulse Bay Hotel (where Orson Welles had missed out on conversing with me).

Even so, it would be decades before the local Chinese took to rugby, in prejudiced Hong Kong.

Police Chief Studholme Wilson

In 1960, when I had just turned 25, I took full advantage of the generous colonial leave system and set out on a six-month around-the-world personal boondoggle!

The management system under the old Empire was by 'tours of duty'. In the early days the tours had been much longer because of sea travel. Now both tours and leaves were shortening, as air flight improved.

My first three-year tour in Hong Kong ended in 1960. I was due six months' paid leave with a return ticket to the UK and spent months planning an incredibly ambitious trip to take me to thirty cities around the world.

As President of the Hong Kong branch of the sixty-nation Junior Chamber International, my pivotal objective was to represent the Colony at its World Congress in Puerto Rico.

On the way there I stayed in Taiwan, Japan, Hawaii, Western Canada, the United States. Then, after the congress, I went up the United States east coast cities to Canada, across to Britain and France, and back via Kenya, Tanganyika, India, Burma, Singapore and Malaysia. Thirty cities.

In those days, that took a lot of correspondence! I arranged friendly accommodation in each city in exchange for a talk and movie promoting the mysterious Hong Kong.

Now I had worldwide contacts for my future career.

* * *

While in African Tanganyika, I had taken local flights to drop in on my sister and brother-in-law at their tea plantation in Njombe, way off in central Africa.

Then, back in civilisation, I stayed in Dar Es Salaam with the last Colonial Commissioner of Police there, *Geoffrey Studholme Wilson, CMG* and *Mrs Studholme Wilson*. It was the final year of that colony's existence in the Empire and I was to experience the euphoria of its domination.

Touring New Zealanders played win-at-all-cost rugby as the Police Chief's son and my pal, Colony rugby star Jeremy Studholme Wilson, discovered in Hong Kong when he was disabled for life a few years later by an illegal scissor tackle by two players coming from different directions at the same time. His sporting days would be over.

His father was appointed to the position in Africa following his dramatic career in Hong Kong which included the Japanese invasion. Jeremy's mother escaped alone to Macau with her two sons, and set off on foot through dangerous wartime China avoiding the Japanese Army, crossing the Himalayas and finding refuge in India. A truly remarkable story!

I spent the visit to Tanganyika acting out as a Colonial Potentate in their palatial, secured police compound and mansion. This was colonial power, living and luxury at its traditional grandest with spacious rooms, ceiling fans, and silently attentive uniformed guards and attendants, stiff in discipline and starched uniforms.

For me personally, it was the apex of my experience as a traditional colonial, but disillusion had already set in on my indoctrinated younger acceptance of the Empire, notwithstanding the advantages the system was bringing to me personally.

Well, I could say apologetically, "That was then, and this is now." But it did not mean I had to just accept or condone the past Empire as I now perceived it.

In 1961, just the next year, Tanganyika became the independent state Tanzania. But things were to change again as soon as 1964, when a rebellion in nearby

Zanzibar, against their traditional Arab oppressors allowed them to merge and create the present United Republic of Tanzania.

Commissioner and Mrs Studholme Wilson had retired gratefully and unconcerned to their estate in sunny South Portugal.

Taipan Hugh Barton

Finally, back in the Hong Kong in the early 1960s, I could see great economic change happening.

The Hong Kong industrial era was getting underway, driven by businessmen fleeing Communist oppression in China. There was available labour, cheap products and especially plastics industries beginning to build prosperity. Hong Kong was becoming increasingly independent but there was yet no legal trade across the border.

China was still absent and Hong Kong isolated, but increased air travel and tourism were starting to make their mark. Today more than thirty award-winning hotels and resorts are proudly operated under the international Mandarin Oriental Hotels luxury banner. Then a modern hotel in Hong Kong was just a dream.

* * *

The Hong Kong Jardine Taipan, *The Hon. Hugh Barton,* was tall and imposing. He had taken over Jardine from my benefactor *Sir John Keswick.* Thin on top and at the end of his career, he still had a twinkle in his eye and a fine tenor voice. He was approachable and chatty but always the regal Jardine Taipan.

He alone saw a big future in tourism and stubbornly wanted a hotel to replace the ancient Queen's Building. What Hugh wanted, Hugh got.

A lone, brave voice at the board meetings against the hotel concept was traditionalist *Bevan Field MC,* a war hero with a meritorious Military Cross in the defence of Hong Kong. He had bullet wound scars on his throat and a weak voice to prove it. A shy, self-effacing demeanour was belied by his determined eyes. He was socially reclusive, having committed the unforgivable social sin then of consorting too enthusiastically with his pretty family Chinese nanny, and more importantly being caught out with her, causing his popular wife to leave him and head back to England in a huff, never to return.

But although the Land Company was a widely held public company, Jardine controlled the board and a hotel was inevitable. Bevan had tactlessly awarded too many contracts to Jardine's competitors or he could have weathered the storm.

His retirement to a board position was announced. My easy-going, heavy-drinking pal *Vernon Roberts* had no ethical qualms and became manager, jumping to unexpected celebrity status overnight and building the first Mandarin Hotel.

Having fun designing the hotel, we hired internationally renowned, interior and set designer *Don Ashton*. He was urbane and polished. His public rooms turned out colourful and stunning. The finished Mandarin well exceeded the standards existing in Hong Kong at the time.

Gerard Henderson, a flamboyant, internationally known young Eurasian artist, furiously painted the wall panels. He worked energetically in the steaming Hong Kong summer, naked but for a wildly swinging thong, in a chaotic, paint-splattered studio I had arranged for him. I still have the 'rent' panel he painted for me while we chugged wine together.

The first Mandarin Hotel fully opened early in 1964, but the Hon. Hugh Barton had ironically long retired!

* * *

By the time of the first Mandarin, I was personally well established in the Colonial business society. But I knew nothing of China. It was still that mysterious, massive, quiet country over our horizon. Obviously, *Mao Tse-tsung's* continuous attempts at development were not working and the country was more or less still isolated.

In 1961 they had created a stir by attacking India and causing the Border Wars and they had no compunction about having annexed Tibet.

In 1963 they had established their technical ability by exploding an atomic bomb.

They were boasting that their Second Economic Plan was successful and producing more material goods. However, the turmoil caused by Mao's Great Leap Forward, although officially ended in 1961, appeared to have really stagnated all development activity in the country.

In Hong Kong, China continued to be missing!

All Blacks Clarke and Meads

Social life in the Colony for us colonials evolved around the expatriate society, for me particularly through rugby and the Football Club.

Our international sphere of the game was expanding rapidly, from Japan down to Singapore, and tours to other countries away from the restrictions of island life in Hong Kong were always very welcomed.

The prospects of international tours received a big boost when *President Sukarno* of Indonesia started a war. He was apparently in an expansionist mood and had been flexing his muscles.

Indonesia had been taken over by the Dutch, who beat the British to it, as long ago as 1596, and finally got independence in 1945. Already sporting a big population and the world's largest archipelago, Sukarno was intent upon taking over more land and had been making moves on what is now Malaysia.

Allies of the British Empire came to then Malaya's assistance and certainly the presence of the British Naval base in Singapore was vital. Military forces were provided Malaya from Australia and New Zealand, bringing powerful rugby to the region!

I had played for Hong Kong against their Commonwealth Brigade All-Star team, and they invited us back to their main military camp in Malaya. We set off way too enthusiastically.

We stopped first in Bangkok and lost to the Thailand national team (all Thais) in their large stadium. They had acted unfairly and we discovered the 'players' with whom we had wildly partied late into the previous night (and Thais *can* party) were not the same players we faced on the field the next day!

We limped away and took a military plane to the Malayan jungle.

Deep in the hills we were of course annihilate by the mighty Anzac rugby selection who were tough and fielding several international Anzac rugby stars. They were also literally fighting fit, conducting a real war, mopping up invasions and engaging in actual hard combat in Malaya and Brunei. We were of course soundly beaten in the games.

Finally, we ended up technically in the middle of the war, in urban Singapore taking our revenge by beating up the team of mainly local Singaporeans and partying for days.

Still, President Sukarno was not totally serious, never stepping outside safe Indonesia, only calling it a 'confrontation' and eventually pulling out of the fight in 1966.

* * *

In the early sixties repeated concussions had forced me out of the game and I was relegated to a voluntary desk job running the Rugby Union as Hon. Secretary.

Arising from those earlier jungle Down-Under friendships, as Union secretary I was able to convince the mighty New Zealand All Black national rugby team, to visit Hong Kong for a stopover 'training session' in 1963 on its way to Europe.

They were the leading rugby team in the world, and this was a great public relations coupe for Hong Kong's early tourism industry. We of course put them into The Mandarin Hotel!

The All Blacks attracted the largest crowd so far seen at a rugby event in Hong Kong. We were disappointed there was no game but fascinated by the commentary on the training session and players, kindly provided by Kiwi journalists travelling with the team.

Just to watch internationally famous 'The Boot' *Don Clarke* practising his kicking, *Colin Meads* marshalling his forwards, or *Kevin Briscoe* getting his backs running was enough!

Their manager *Frank Kilby* was apologetic they could not play but thank heavens they did not. The Colony team would have been totally outclassed. Their short visit did put Hong Kong on the serious international rugby map.

The mighty All Blacks were pictured around the world in the Football Club stadium. "They actually have a stadium and hotels in Hong Kong?"

At least international rugby had arrived in Hong Kong, although culture and entertainment generally were slow to arrive!

With increasing stability and commerce Hong Kong was joining the world and beginning to attract well-known artists, shows and entertainment.

We were surprised to see *Frank Sinatra* and entourage seated at the next table one late evening after a tour show and shouted our inebriated greetings. We attended *The Beatles* and *Louis Armstrong* as mentioned elsewhere. But overall, club bands were Filipino or standard nightclub groups on contract, playing old staples.

I was beginning to be complacent with my way of life. Little did I know that I was missing those brilliant 1960s in Britain, its social highpoint of the century. And I was not experiencing the political transition of the Western world during that time, especially of racism in America.

Back there in Britain, although they were in debt up to their ears, the nation was totally oblivious to their circumstances. Everyone appeared to be active, enjoying the full employment, and their manufacturing was still leading the world, before the rise of Japan and China as industrial powers. Working people in the UK were better off than ever before.

Consequently, the country was deluged in new creation and the cultural revolution was under way: *Rolling Stones, Beatles, Dave Clark Five, Twiggy, Mary Quant* and the mini skirt, *Elizabeth Taylor* and *Sean Connery* for a start.

Socially, the United Kingdom progressed: liberalising gambling, homosexuality, divorce, abortion and other previously regulated activities. Party time!

America had been dismayed by Russia's successful launch of Sputnik, the first satellite, in 1957, causing *President John F. Kennedy* to retaliate with the Apollo programme. He was not to see the triumphant landing of the first men on the Moon at the end of the decade due to his tragic assassination in 1963.

It was the time in America of the civil rights movement, anti-war demonstrations, the generation gap, pop culture, the age of Aquarius and of freedom-claiming hippies. Of *Manson, Andy Warhol, Grace Kelly, Elvis Presley, Jane Fonda, Joan Baez, John Wayne* and many more. Generally, the pop culture thrived despite the threats of racism and violence.

Internationally came *Sophia Loren, Eartha Kitt, Maurice Chevalier, Grace Kelly, Catherine Deneuve* and so on. It was the stimulating time of *Marilyn Monroe, Brigitte Bardot* and of increasing titillating, obscured forbidden sex scenes and flashes of nudity.

I was unknowingly missing the most upbeat decade of the century, tucked away in an isolated self-satisfied little parochial enclave, even isolated from China itself, dull and unexciting as it was at that stage of its restricting Communist development.

The Steele-Perkins

Wing Commander Horace Steele-Perkins made a name for himself in the Colony, due to the sexy *Mimi Lau*. This happened way before the Japanese invasion in 1941. Many British fellows had pretty Chinese girls hidden away. But Mimi was associated with the construction company Horace, employed to build the Hong Kong defences.

A double no-no: being caught out publicly with his pants down was bad enough. Being associated with a financial scandal was almost worse. Many expatriates profited from corrupt Asia business, but appearances had to be maintained! Back then, letting the side down did in Horace.

Mimi Lau was still active when I was in Hong Kong. And I was about to marry into that Steele-Perkins family!

* * *

The 'Virgins' Retreat' on Garden Road in Hong Kong was formally The Helena May Institute for Young Ladies. Newly arriving colonial females slept there in safety before released to the pack of suitable male predators lurking by the gate.

"You won't believe it," whispered the stern mature manageress. "There is another Steele-Perkins in town! And she is staying here."

Uncle Horace never met me, but I knew the highly respected uncle *Dr Sir Derek Steele-Perkins*, who restored the family good name as head of the Admiralty medical service and a personal physician to the Queen. More important he played rugby for the Navy!

His brother *Dr Jan Steele-Perkins* was the eye surgeon in the Bahamas and his daughter Vanessa was the young woman who had arrived at the Helena May – and whom I was to marry – from far away in yet another colony of the Empire, The Bahamas.

* * *

The Bahamian Islands, still totally under British control in the mid 1960s, buzzed with thousands of tourists. The majority black population was evident in all walks of life and ready to take control. But the social clubs were still exclusively white – the Sailing Club, the Government House Tennis Club, the Golf Club and inside the gated and fenced Lyford Cay!

Developed from bush at the west end by Canadian developer *E.P.Taylor*, Lyford Cay was the home of the international super rich and of a few leading white Bahamian families. Most senior colonials still lived out east in their beautiful sun-filled mansions and gardens. They were increasingly worried about crime from 'Over the Hill' where the black population lived in relative poverty, chafing for independence.

The Steele-Perkins family was very racially liberal and introduced me to many of their friends in the black community. Her father, a champion golfer, had personally opened the first mixed-race golf course in the colony.

We were there over Christmas and invited to the home of *Sir Roland* and *Lady Simonette* to celebrate. The recently appointed Premier of the Bahamas had just negotiated internal self-government.

'Pop', as his family called him, was a relaxed, self-taught island boy. He led the singing around his grand piano – as one would expect of a preacher's son – with gusto, assuming us dutifully to know the words to belt out Christmas carols.

Sir Roland claimed the highest of ethical values. Nevertheless, just business of course, but he had become the richest man in the Bahamas through whiskey running during the American Prohibition. He had invested those gains in real estate and multiple businesses, even in those days being proclaimed a billionaire.

He was held in high regard by the Americans having played by the book, never moving into American waters where Prohibition applied, but he had also cooperated with the American authorities from time to time and became open partners with the renowned Canadian bootlegging Bronfman distillery.

He was a very friendly outgoing fellow and he bumped into me several times during my visits to the Bahamas. He served more than 50 years in their parliament, essentially protecting The Bay Street Boys and business interests, during which he saw the Bahamas through to full independence.

Worries about rioting were common at the Royal Nassau Sailing Club bar. "What will we do when they come marching over the hill?" As a middle-class English guy, I was just an observer watching the English colonial elite finally getting their comeuppance. And we could just fly away.

But first I had to earn my trip. Their northern island of Grand

Bahama was the latest international sensation in the growing post-War tourist industry.

Our shopping centre tenants in Hong Kong were interested in renting space in another colony on the other side of the world and while I was in the area, I was asked to do a survey.

I took my notebook and importantly hired a small plane flight at my company's expense to make my assessment. The small island was ripped apart by construction activity. The strip hotels were packed with workers and indeed they could boast the zero vacancy which had attracted attention on the other side of the world. But at least for the seeable future it was feeding on itself and although eager to return, I had to recommend investment restraint. Wait and see.

The island and its port went through a series of convulsions, before succeeding, including an attempt at self-independence.

Half a century later its major investor is the Hutchinson group from Hong Kong, with whom my partner Stanley Kwok has remained closely associated.

***

We completed an around-the-world trip and returned to a new prestigious home way up on The Peak in Hong Kong, courtesy of The Land Company.

Property Taipan Vernon Roberts

I had learned that the colonial systems established under the Empire were based upon violence, control and self-interest, which really goes without saying. Everything taken by force, even if restrained or threatened, results in dominated and servient people.

The degree by which this was applied depended upon the situation, and I saw these systems in their variations in Africa, the Middle East throughout Asia and indeed North America. By my generation the use of overt force was more subtle. Still, while Britannia ruled the waves, British colonialists like me still thrived supreme.

***

China is an ancient and distinct civilisation. Hong Kong was a curious mixture of uppity Brits and equally self-confident Chinese plus highly successful, mixed-race and Middle-Eastern people, who had no sense of inferiority; usually quite the opposite!

Hong Kong colonialism subtly adopted the Asian system of bribery and payoffs in the background, but always there, hidden behind polite conversation and those discrete cocktail parties. As always, the Empire builders threw themselves enthusiastically into the unethical fray, retiring to respectability and English rose-covered cottages.

Locals and senior expatriates were now offering me significant inducements for favours. I indignantly threw out a dining friend who nonchalantly offered me a substantial sum to pre-leak specifications to his bidding company.

Within the local neighbourhood police itself bribery was public knowledge. Later, in 1977, the Governor was finally forced publicly into an amnesty with the police force forgiving all past corruption, just to keep the system operating.

* * *

At the Land Company my pal, the cavalier Vernon Roberts settled in as manager of one of the most important companies in the colony. His ebullient wife Linda had died young from their excessive life and Vernon had married a stunningly beautiful young American blonde … as was expected of him.

Vernon had already announced I had "the highest likelihood of succeeding him as general manager in due course", perhaps to keep me around, and hinted at my inheriting his magnificent company mansion on Shouson Hill. He wrote me a glowing report (after all he was a pal and likely tipsy at the time!).

Thus, things were going well in Hong Kong. Now a senior, the 'right people' sought *me,* and I was getting big financial kickback proposals in common with the Asian way of doing business. My life was a continuous round of business entertaining, I was drinking far too much. I decided to slow down and to start a law degree!

London University accepted me in External Law, and I enrolled, part-time, at Hong Kong University, continued later in England and completed the degree in Canada. All the time I worked full-time, travelled extensively and never took a lecture or correspondence course.

I analysed the curriculum for each year, acquired the past examination papers, broke the questions down into weighted probabilities, and bought all the necessary textbooks. To simplify final revision, I physically cut out all the unnecessary chapters!

At the beginning of my studies, I had a bachelor apartment but when I finally graduated with honours in Canada, I was in a splendid semi-waterfront home with little kids banging on my study door. It was a long effort!

But in Hong Kong I was now married, already with a son, and we had decided the Hong Kong way of life was not for us. We had seen the civilised world out there and it beckoned.

* * *

Should I have stayed? Four decades later, my wife Lane Middleton and I were visiting Hong Kong. We had lunch with a retired senior Land Company lawyer, and I asked what happened to the Shouson Hill mansion I might have inherited had I stayed. She chuckled, "We eventually demolished it to build an apartment block and found a considerable stash of hidden gold bars which have never been claimed. How do you account for that?"

Yes, perhaps I should indeed have stayed!

My mentor Vernon and the Land Company successfully went on to ride an expanding business cycle, only for him to die suddenly in his fifties, undoubtedly from the excessive life!

Trevor Bedford, a close rugger friend of mine, had taken the job I might have assumed. He enjoyed a period of roaring success to become one of Hong Kong's pre-eminent businessmen. Then he was caught, dramatically over-financed, by the severe 1980s high interest rates. Helpful colonial banks saved the Land Company and possibly Jardine itself from bankruptcy, but Trevor and the then *Jardine Taipan, David Newbigging* both lost their jobs and disappeared back to the UK. David recovered splendidly later saving Lloyds Insurance and becoming *Sir David*!

* * *

We packed our bags and left Hong Kong in 1966, opting, to the company's annoyance, under my outdated contract, for a long and expensive first-class family luxury cruise back to the UK. This would have amused *Sir John Keswick* who wrote my original contract and insisted I travel by sea to become a true Colonial.

My time in Hong Kong had drawn to an end. The coast of Asia was no longer isolated or quiet.

When I had arrived in 1958 the Great Famine was commencing

in Communist China and as I left in 1966, *Mao Tse-tung* launched his debilitating Great Proletarian Cultural Revolution.

America had started its disastrous war in Vietnam against the spread of Communism.

Then there were the Elsie Elliott riots in Hong Kong, promoted by the Red Guards from Communist China, commencing a wave of emigration which would impact upon my future life. But this time I was heading away from the colony's mounting problems.

Reality

I had been happily waving the Union Jack for Britain as an isolated Colonialist for approaching a decade, but during that time a staggering number of countries had pulled out of the Empire. I was heading back to reality.

So far through the 1960s, while I was in Hong Kong, the Empire had lost Aden, Cypress, Nigeria, Kuwait, Somaliland, Tanganyika, Sierra Leone, Jamaica, Trinidad and Tobago, Kenya, Malawi, Malta, Uganda, Maldives, Zambia, Guyana, Botswana, Rhodesia, Lesoto, Gambia, Zanzibar and Barbados.

I was returning to a very much more chastened post-Empire Britain.

The Duke of Westminster

Now I was making it in the privileged world, things had a way of sorting themselves out more easily!

Back in England, a friend, *Sir Bill Ramsay,* who had chaired the English Rugby Football Union, and *Lady Nora*, casually asked, "Why not stay in our cottage at Reigate on the south coast while His Grace gets to know you?"

But would I join the prestigious Grosvenor Estate and go on to their international office in Vancouver?

I had to make a difficult decision. Go to Canada in the New World or finish my law degree and continue as a barrister in London. I was accepted as a student at Inner Temple and could start 'dinners', their ancient tradition. It was an intriguing decision.

Then Grosvenor offered me terms I could not refuse! The family went back a thousand years when *Hugh Lupus Gros Veneur,* accompanied

William the Conqueror and was given the north-west of England as his part of the spoils to protect their new empire from the Scottish and Welsh savages. I still considered them savages, but perhaps because mine were encountered on the rugby pitch.

* * *

Grosvenor's extensive land and property holdings in the prime centre of London in Mayfair and surrounding areas, derived from the marriage of a Grosvenor to *Mary Davis*, daughter of a wealthy city merchant. In the 1700s they famously developed the rough land into Mayfair, Belgravia, and Victoria, into some of the world's most valuable real estate.

I visited their properties in, what had been, England's earliest and longest colony, Ireland. They were thrown out of most of the island in 1922 and that year proved a critical turning point for the British Empire. Much worse was to come! The Grosvenors however retained their Irish estates in splendid affluence.

* * *

Now they had also become active around the globe. After World War Two, money movement was restricted out of the United Kingdom, but Grosvenor were permitted to develop Annacis Island, near New Westminster, British Columbia 'to help the Canadian economy'. The Bank of England erroneously assumed New Westminster was a Duke of Westminster estate, misled by the scheming Premier of British Columbia, W.A.C. 'Wacky' Bennett.

In Vancouver, Grosvenor had formed a partnership with the Canadian Pacific Railway to develop the entire central waterfront of Vancouver, then docks and rail tracks, as Project 200, a massive urban development and one of the biggest in North America.

Grosvenor knew I worked on developing major properties on the Hong Kong waterfront and offered me a seat on the Grosvenor International board and management of Project 200 under their international chief, Canadian Gilbert Hardman.

It was a wonderful, very high-paying opportunity and Gilbert met me in London for a final interview at the Connaught Hotel, of course a Grosvenor property, in Mayfair itself.

I was barely acknowledged by the reclusive, country-gentleman Duke, but I dutifully visited all the Grosvenor Estate properties, cheered on His Grace's prize racehorse Arkle and joined in endless lunches, dinners and meetings.

* * *

I had visited Canada several times but knew few details. I decided to do some research. As a schoolboy in the east of England I was aware that the Vikings left us mythology of a great land over the seas far beyond the horizon to the west. Christopher Columbus in 1492 and all that, were part of our culture but I learned that our randy old King Henry VIII had quickly commissioned John Cabot to discover Newfoundland around then and then Cape Breton.

None other than Sir Francis Drake likely saw Vancouver Island during his 1500s sailing holiday around the world. But by then England had moved successfully into the colonial land acquisition business.

All it then took was to fill in the middle Canadian bit: Great Lakes, the Shield, the Prairies, the Rockies and to 'discover' the frozen North.

English schoolchildren knew the tale that Champlain had built a fort at Quebec City for France to control the St Lawrence River, only for them to essentially lose the whole country when two young generals met in a brief storybook skirmish on the Plains of Abraham and showing remarkable lack of personal capability, managed to kill each other.

Then all it took was more Hudsons Bay trading, a couple of gold rushes, crossing the Rockies and Wild West railways to complete the acquisition.

Possibly ten thousand years earlier the ancestors of Canada's scattered indigenous people crossed the Bering Strait land bridge and spread out and down the west coast and across the continent. As was the practice in the entire British Empire, it was also necessary to negotiate or impose some sort of deal, convenient for us, with the folk we discovered.

The indigenous peoples and their possessions went with the forced possession of the entire territory, and they were now, like all equal citizens of Canada, subjects of the Sovereign Crown, if somewhat reluctantly.

This sovereignty principle had been 'legalised' internationally by the Peace of West Phalia in 1647 when the warring European nations established the self-serving principle of mutual non-interference based upon their inalienable right to physically possess territories. This principle was modernised into international law in the United Nations Charter of 1945 assuring 'the right to authority, supremacy and territoriality'.

The Queen, Mounties and beavers! That all sounded safe enough, so I made my final deal with Grosvenor, packed bags, thanked Sir Bill and Lady Nora for the use of their cottage and their local pub, and in 1967 headed off expectantly to discover Canada.

Mayor Tom Terrific

We flew in style to Vancouver, were met by a young English colleague (much later to become *Sir Michael Ridley* for real estate service to the Crown). We had a smart home provided in a posh area and a car waiting in the garage. I was 32. It was a first-class arrival all around and we were to become Canadian!

Even then the correct 'Victorian' ways of the Empire were still evident in Vancouver. All bars and most shops were closed on the Sabbath. "What is a Sabbath?" ask my grandchildren.

Even drinking wine or alcohol in the garden was not permitted if you could be seen from the street. Taverns still had 'Men' and 'Women' entrances and bars. There was almost no outdoor fun restaurant dining.

All the exclusive business and sports clubs were white and catered to males only. And come to that were exclusively Christian. Anyone who was different or observed to have a dusky skin had only been legally able to become a citizen for twenty years and in real life white male supremacy still dominated.

Homosexuality was still illegal. Only a hundred years earlier, until 1869, the penalty had technically been death!

With sound Canadian logic, the gross indecency law had been extended to include intimate relationships between women as recently as 1953, in the interest of equality.

Very soon after we arrived, however, in 1969 'sodomy and gross indecency' laws were changed allowing 'such acts' under some circumstances. Remarkably, it would be twenty years before the criminal code repealed all these 'offences' completely.

At the time, when we arrived in 1967, however, these ideas also applied to much of the world.

* * *

I was surprised upon arrival to realise that such a remarkably large county as Canada was still not independent of Great Britain.

The British North America Act had unified Canada in 1867, but left final control in the hands of the Mother Country. Right up until 1949 the Supreme Court of Canada had been subordinated to the Privy Council in the United Kingdom.

While essentially internally self-governing, Canada could not change its constitution under the ancient BNA Act without approval from Britain, and the federal and provincial governments had been arguing about it among themselves for many decades.

In the meantime I was coming to a country still under the final control of Great Britain. Not quite the same as a colony, but I was still serving my Empire!

* * *

I went straight to work. *Bill Graham*, the prominent Vancouver City Planner was my first contact to discuss the detailed layout of the entire Project 200 plan. The outline had been enthusiastically endorsed by the City Council a few months previously.

The highly ambitious, vast development would build a double-stacked freeway along the entire Vancouver waterfront, starting at Stanley Park and eventually linking up with the intended Trans-Canada Highway to the east of the city.

It could happen because Canadian Pacific owned tracks dominating the waterfront, forty feet below the existing street level of the city. On a massive concrete platform, we would build a major shopping centre and mixed-use high-rise buildings, all linked into the central transportation system. It was modelled on the principle of the futuristic Place Ville Marie in Montreal.

The largest planned urban development in North America, it was an awe-inspiring modern design. The city would provide major financing and the popular Mayor Tom Campbell, known in the press as Tom Terrific, enthusiastically supported the development.

He was something of an eccentric character, rushing excitedly from meeting to meeting and always short of time. One could easily imagine him jumping from building to building in a Superman-style outfit complete with cape!

Provincial Premier 'Wacky' Bennett and the Federal government were to bear most of the freeway cost.

Tom Terrific meet me frequently at meetings during those early months in Canada. He was flamboyant and outspoken, tending to make strong, intense eye contact, dominating the discussion. Typical of the times, he had personal real estate investments in central Vancouver benefitting him directly from his decisions.

* * *

I was thirty-two and we had bought a new three-bedroom rancher on half an acre near the waterfront in smart West Vancouver for my entire $21,000 cash savings!

In those days home telephones hung on the wall in the kitchen. I vividly recall a Sunday morning about a year later, answering the phone and hearing *City Planner Bill Graham* almost in tears shouting, "Project 200 is dead!" Tom Campbell had just told him the Feds and Province had pulled out financially!

On Monday morning Gilbert and I rushed to City Hall, but the mayor was adamant. That was the end of Project 200.

Tom Terrific switched immediately to personally promoting and supporting Pacific Centre, a proposed major mid-town shopping complex. That period also saw the end of the flamboyant mayor's political life when he called out the police to violently quell a dopey, hippy, pot-smoking 'riot' in Gastown, completing his career in infamy.

Shocked at the loss of Project 200, I moved on to developing Guildford Town Centre and the Mayfair Shopping Centre in Victoria, justifying my continued stay in Canada.

Vancouver fortunately never did bring any freeways within central city boundaries but instead widened and upgraded existing main roads. This turned out to be absolutely the right decision, retaining the character and preserving at grade access to the entire waterfront when the rail tracks were removed. Project 200 would have been disastrous for the city.

But this was the reason we were in Vancouver!

The young Gerald Grosvenor

The eighteen-year-old Grosvenor Estate heir, *Gerald Grosvenor,* arrived in Vancouver, as he excitedly said, "For a cowboy adventure."

He was in training to become one of the richest men in the world.

Chunky Woodward, with whom we worked closely, owned the famous, vast Woodwards Ranch, and his Woodward's department stores were key tenants in each of our new shopping centres.

We were warned by the London Office that young Gerald, straight from Harrow school, was not 'very worldly' and not accustomed to paying for anything.

I was assigned to look after him and spent a few days showing him around the city and getting him outfitted for the 'cowboy boots' he was obsessing about. We spent several hours at the Army and Navy Store fitting boots, jeans and designer shirts, and buying a big backpack he found novel and amusing.

He never reached into his pocket to take out a wallet, if he indeed possessed one, or even thought about the need to pay. At the suggestion of Head Office, a modest waterfront hotel had been selected for him on English Bay, but we were warned he would just walk out!

At the bus station, going to the ranch, we bought him a return ticket, explaining the need to retain the return part, and put dollars in his pocket for food and drink on the way. He happily waved good-bye as the bus left for the long journey inland to Merritt. He was a charming, rather shy but friendly young fellow already chatting with those around him. On return he said he had a great time at the ranch 'being a cowboy'.

Gerald became The Duke of Westminster and one of the richest people in Britain. A decade later he had not forgotten. He invited us to his post-wedding reception in Vancouver in his early happy days with Natalia and included me occasionally in events when he was in town. Twenty-five years later, I was chair of a real estate conference in Vancouver, and I invited him to be the keynote evening speaker. Always charming, he accepted readily.

Architect Dr Stanley Kwok

Gilbert Hardman finally overstepped himself. With Project 200 gone, the Grosvenor London Office reduced the ambitious Vancouver set-up and called me back to the UK.

However, I decided to stay in Canada. Canadian Industries Limited, a subsidiary of the then mighty Imperial Chemical Industries in Britain, had asked me to start an international property investment group for them in North America. They offered an irresistible substantial equity interest.

My requirement was that it be run from Vancouver and that I continue travelling and living the first-class life, to which my colonial experience had accustomed me.

Thus, in 1970 I said goodbye to Grosvenor and opened my own office, Canadian Freehold Properties Ltd.

We were immediately in business. I initially did a survey of all their real estate in North America and in Asia, and we took over ownership of those with latent redevelopment value, without any debt. We were then able to use those assets as security for new market purchases before redeveloping them themselves, when their industrial activity had been relocated. The company was successful and expanded quickly.

* * *

Stanley Kwok had entered my life in Hong Kong, way back in 1958. He was already a partner in the leading architectural firm, Eric Cumine and Associates, and examiner at the University of Hong Kong.

Stanley's young wife Eleanor died suddenly in the Hong Kong polio epidemic in the 1950s, leaving him with two children. He was then a swinging bachelor driving around town in a Mercedes sports car. When I left Hong Kong, he was a big-name designer of significant projects and famous for opening the first trendy espresso coffee shop.

He married Mim, gave up all that status and moved to a new life in Vancouver. I introduced him to Grosvenor during Hardman's heady days, so we had already worked together. We were about to form a partnership and lifetime friendship.

Stanley joined me with an ownership in Freehold. We invited in major pension funds, particularly the powerful ICI Pension Fund from the UK, giving us international connections. Pension funds were just then realising the bond-like characteristics of prime real estate investment. Over the next decade we built a large real estate group with international properties.

* * *

"Getting to Yes" was our mantra, based on Harvard professor *Dr Roger Fisher's* famous thesis by that name. We had a fun-loving and close team in the seventies when friendly relationships and fun office parties could still be risked in business.

When *Dr Fisher* met me, I had been impressed by his lecture while promoting his book *Musts and Wants*, which first established 'Must Haves' and then placed value counts upon 'Would Likes'. You just add up the results and you have your logical solution.

The celebrity lecturer, Dr Fisher enjoyed a remarkable career as a negotiation and conflict resolution expert. He told me he had advised *President Nixon* on strategy for imminent talks with the Soviet Union to restrict the development of nuclear arms.

During their first meeting in the Oval Office the President sat behind his desk annoyed at one of his celebrated dogs which was sitting on the carpet near Dr Fisher chewing hard at the fringe. "Bad dog," shouted the President. "Stop chewing the carpet and come here," opening a lower drawer, giving the dog a biscuit, and patting him for his obedience.

The President was about to bargain with the aggressive Russians. Dr Fisher sighed and pointed out to that he was rewarding his dog for chewing the carpet. Nixon waved his hand in amused dismissal.

The Trudeaus

We could see Margaret Trudeau down on the street being threatened, crying out frantically for help, and begging for mercy. I tried to convince her father to rush down, but he shook his head decisively!

* * *

The Hon. James Sinclair, Margaret Trudeau's father, came emphatically into my life at the beginning of the 1970s. Jimmy Sinclair had been a federal cabinet minister but was now a wealthy Vancouver businessman on the boards of companies such as the Bank of Montreal and Canadian Industries Limited.

His personality and sparkling humour dominated the room. He was born in Scotland, then his family emigrated and he went to university in Vancouver. He got a Rhodes Scholarship back to Oxford and did postgraduate work at Princeton. A bright guy!

Jimmy was already in his mid-sixties when he met me. He and his wife Kathleen lived nearby in British Properties, with their five daughters. Everything was calm until their attractive 18-year-old flower child *Margaret* met *Pierre Elliott Trudeau* on a family holiday in Tahiti.

The charming and debonair Trudeau was 47 at the time and Canada's Minister of Justice, although the young Margaret may well not have bothered much about that. Anyway, why would she? He was about the same age as her mother!

I attended many public functions and like thousands I had shaken his hand and seen Pierre Trudeau in action. Jimmy was becoming my acquaintance, just when Pierre and Margaret married secretly in 1971.

Jimmy was on our parent CIL's board and our designated director.

I saw a lot of him during Margaret's entire drama-filled, short marriage. We travelled to Montreal for meetings and stayed together in hotels, often having casual meals together.

The Trudeau courtship and wedding was in secret, and the small reception was at our Capilano Golf Club where we dined occasionally with Jimmy and Kathleen to entertain visiting businesspeople. We talked, as people do, about our families and his successful daughters, but the subject of Margaret and Pierre was avoided, especially after her wild party with The Rolling Stones in Toronto. Her six-year tumultuous life with Trudeau came to an end in separation by 1977.

At breakfast on the top floor of the Chateau Champlain in Montreal, Jimmy called me to the window and pointed way down into the street where there was a commotion. "Look," he said, "Margaret is making a movie down there."

He had at last raised the forbidden subject, and as we had to walk that way to the office, I proposed dropping by. Jimmy just gave me a pained look and that was the end of that. Margaret lost her chance of making my acquaintance.

The Guardian Angel; L'ange gardien, a romantic comedy, was released in 1978 to quite good reviews,

* * *

Thirty years later, my other indirect Trudeau connection comes through my politically minded wife Lane, who is not however a Federal Liberal and adamantly denies any personal Trudeau relationship.

She cannot avoid the fact that her talented niece, Dr Sarah Tarshis of McGill University, is married to the journalist Sam Trudeau and they produced the energetic little Jacob Trudeau. So, whatever she says about politics, Lane is indirectly connected to the Trudeaus.

However she admits she enjoyed her one conversation with *Pierre Elliott Trudeau.* They shared the same birthdate, October 18, and being the forward person she is, coming across him in public in Montreal around that date, she went up to wish him a happy birthday. As was his character, he gave her his full charming attention and they had a very pleasant conversation.

"How did you know it was my birthday? Is it yours too?" he asked, carefully turning the conversation back to her and making her feel as if she were the only person in the room. She remembers it all entirely, word for word, such was his renowned charisma.

That has not changed her view of his politics! Lane went to McGill University and spent a career in business leaving her a convinced fiscal Conservative.

In another interesting coincidence, way back in 1977, when I saw Margaret Trudeau movie making, Margaret had moved to 2021 Atwater, a smart Montreal downtown apartment building. Lane was to later live a very happy 20-year apartment life there, while she was employed by Seagram Distilleries.

Then Lane set off on her around-the-world acting aspirations which led her to Vancouver, where she was to meet me in the new century.

Benjie, The Earl of Iveagh

Finally, in 1972, my neighbour Little Benjie Iveagh from Suffolk came into my life. He was now His Lordship the Earl of Iveagh!

Benjamin Guinness inherited the family beer fortunes along with the titles and became chair of the company at the tender age of 25. When first introduced to me, he cordially announced, "Call me Benjie." I did ... cautiously! He was a charming man always ready to listen, always with glass in hand!

When we met he was in his late thirties and already going through a rough time. A close friend, *Peter Finch* ran his companies, British Properties and Park Royal Shopping Centre in West Vancouver, and tactically invited me to meet Benjie socially.

I was Chair of the Municipal Planning Commission with some influence over the development of their estates. But more, as we got to know each other, he talked to me as a Canadian fellow developer.

I had been President of the national Community Planning

Association of Canada, grandly flying around the country chairing conferences and dealing with city planning issues. My tennis partner *Peter Jones*, who was *Mayor of West Vancouver* talked me into chairing his local Planning Commission.

* * *

Benjie's father, the Second Brewer Earl, sailed into Vancouver in 1931 on his West Coast yacht and snapped up 4000 acres of mountainside from the bankrupt West Vancouver for a song.

Proceeds from his Guinness Beer business then built the Lions Gate Suspension Bridge, linking his land to the City of Vancouver, immediately creating a valuable suburb. They then built Canada's first shopping centre, in West Vancouver, Park Royal. My friend Peter had the cushy job of managing all these properties and especially keeping Benjie's glass full. At least Peter had Finch Hill in West Vancouver named for him!

Back in Ireland things were in a muddle. Benjie proved too inexperienced for chairmanship at 25 and by the time he met me, he had experienced years of disaster. His plan to diversify the company from brewing bought failure after failure. Their public stock price dropped dramatically.

A decade later, reportedly handicapped by his understandable alcoholic intake, he made his most memorable mistake in appointing a shifty fellow called Ernest Saunders to run the company. He apparently allowed Saunders enough latitude to commit major fraud in 1986 when buying Scotch Whiskey producer Distillers, sending Saunders to jail and temporarily devastating Guinness's reputation. Benjie died young, in his mid-fifties.

Their distant British Properties continues profitably to expand development westwards undisturbed. Poor Benjie, he was a very pleasant chap.

Tommy Douglas

We all recognised and loved the Canadian political icon *Tommy Douglas.*

I was absolutely delighted when the slight fellow squeezed past me to take the window seat in my regular six-hour business class, Air Canada 850 flight to Montreal.

Tommy had sensibly quit Saskatchewan winters, where as Premier, he was famous for starting Canada's move to universal medical care, and was now MP for sunny, warm Nanaimo in British Columbia. He was leader of the Federal NDP Loyal Opposition to *Pierre Trudeau's* Liberals. He said he was on his way to Ottawa.

He opened a bulky briefcase and spread his papers liberally, chatting nonstop as was his style. A typical politician, he spoke directly to me and appeared interested in my life.

Tommy met lots of people, but this turned out as an auspicious date! It was in October 1970 which should ring a bell for Canadians of a certain age, being the time of the deadly Insurrection in Quebec. Members of the separatist FLQ had kidnapped the provincial deputy premier *Pierre Laporte* and a British diplomat *James Cross.*

Pierre Trudeau's government was intent upon declaring the War Measures Act and Tommy was on his way to an NDP caucus meeting in Ottawa prior to the parliamentary debate.

I mentioned CIL, my parent company, had reported the theft of a truckload of explosives in Quebec. He riffled through his notes and said he had a similar report. He said things looked serious and Mr Trudeau appeared to have little choice but to invoke the Act.

When the plane landed, he had exiting priority, rushing to his Ottawa connection. He gave a cheery wave and that was the last I saw of him. I took a limo downtown, attended a business dinner and returned to my hotel late in the evening, switching on the television news.

There was Tommy, but now eloquently denying Trudeau's need to invoke the War Measures Act, obviously having met his caucus. Such is politics!

Pierre Trudeau did impose the War Measures Act on October 16, 1970, when Tommy made a controversial ill-timed speech in Parliament deploring the action. Pierre Laporte's body was found in a Quebec airport parked car trunk the next day! James Cross was rescued shaken but unharmed on December 3.

Trudeau's action averted further violence and received widespread support. But Tommy's decision and the unfortunate timing of his opposition had been abysmal! Six months later in April 1971, he resigned as NDP leader.

Tommy finished his days in 1986, fittingly in Ottawa, still a national hero. His daughter *Shirley Douglas*, her husband *Donald Sutherland* and son *Keifer* all achieved fame as actors.

Celebrity upon celebrity.

James Cross died *January 6, 2021, in the United Kingdom of Covid, aged 99.*

Intellectual William F. Buckley, Jnr

William Buckley Jnr was generally acknowledged as America's top intellectual, and he was about to meet me!

The redoubtable *Mrs Kathleen Taylor*, Vancouver's leading socialite and philanthropist, had taken a liking to me and snapped me up as a willing workhorse for her British Columbia Red Cross Society.

By 1970 she had me on the provincial Red Cross board as vice president.

Everyone called her Mrs Taylor, with careful, fawning respect. She was super rich!

She fell out with my anti-social ex-wife when she invited her to a Ladies Party and awarded her the honour of Pouring Tea. "I do not pour tea!" was her scornful dismissal.

I was good friends with her son Austin. We enjoyed horses which we stabled at Southlands Riding Club. We continued as lifelong friends, even when later in life, he became a financial tsar far away in Toronto.

Austin had his own stables and a beautiful selection of horses and ponies. He hooted with laughter at my efforts to train our lowly, beautifully natured Appaloosa family horse to polo. She had learned that her safety depended upon staying far away from swinging mallets and flying balls.

* * *

William F. Buckley Jnr was Austin's brother-in-law and an American television personality. He had founded his influential right wing *National Review* in 1953.

He married Austin's sister Patricia and in 1970 he met me at a Taylor family dinner at their prestigious new mansion on The Crescent, in Vancouver.

Notwithstanding its prime location, this property was a comedown for them. Until Austin's father died in 1965 the Taylors had lived at The Shannon Estate, a ten-acre walled gardened property, the last of Vancouver's central Beaux Art three-storey stately homes. It is still there preserved as the social centre facility in a large housing development.

* * *

Mr Buckley was every inch the patrician, wealthy-through-inheritance American. He was gracing insignificant Vancouver with his presence. Austin and I were totally, absolutely, outclassed!

Austin was the bad boy of the family, having dropped out of the local university and then Princeton before marrying his vivacious, sexy wife Betsie. They disappeared off to Asia, settling in Manila from 1959 to 1963 while I was in Hong Kong.

There he had been beaten almost to death in a business 'misunderstanding'. He had returned when his estranged father died and was working back in the Canadian establishment, at financial company McLeod Young Weir.

William Buckley was, by contrast, every rich father's dream. An officer in the US Army during the Second World War, excelling at Yale as a skilled debater, and writing his first book of fifty, *God and Man*. All before joining the CIA!

He later edited the *National Review* and had a moderately right wing, libertarian national TV show. He is now claimed as the most important public intellectual of his generation. No wonder I was slightly overwhelmed, but he appeared not to faze out big Austin.

* * *

'Bill', which Austin insisted on calling him, retired with us to the library for after-dinner brandy, as gentlemen did in those days, to chat about men's serious things – business and politics. Bill dominated the conversation, but I was in awe just listening to him, knocking back the deceased Mr Taylor's excellent cognac.

Bill mentioned his recent book, *Up from Liberalism*. Austin was over 300 pounds and six feet four tall, with the schoolboy nickname Firpo, (a famous and massive wrestler) shamed me by taunting in his booming voice, "You haven't read it?"

He handed it from the bookcase shaking his head in scorn. Of course, Austin never read it himself.

* * *

Mrs Taylor had 'invited' Bill to Vancouver, to speak at the AGM and fundraiser for the Red Cross. His public affairs, *Firing Line* TV show was one of the most popular in the United States and western world. He was an incredible draw and our Red Cross event sold out at exorbitant ticket prices.

In conversation he spoke with his very refined Bostonian style accent and threw in uncommon words nonchalantly, appearing sometimes to talk in riddles, but successfully establishing his intellectual superiority.

His speech to the Red Cross event was, however, straight forward and well applauded. Austin had to attend but appeared to be snoozing quietly in his seat.

With considerable wealth, Austin Taylor become a national celerity himself. He moved to Toronto in 1977 with his always bubbly wife Elizabeth Taylor (not that one; Betsie), taking over money managers McLeod Young Weir. They had over two thousand employees in forty offices in Canada and branches extensively around the world, who all soon knew approachable Austin.

He once subscribed me for a new share issue without telling me, sold the shares later at a then remarkable profit to me and sent me a cheque. I assume if it had lost money, I would never have heard about it! He was nothing if not self-confident – and rich!

When in Toronto the start to my day was often personal jugs (literally!) of coffee and enormous sticky buns in his early morning office to hear the state of the economy.

By the mid-1980s he was over 350 pounds. He imported a London taxi as his chauffeur-driven limo so he could lie down on his back and slide out the wide door. My last lunch with him was at a favourite Toronto Italian restaurant. He lumbered into our large booth, selected the red wine as always without consultation, ordering loudly, "A bottle for me and a bottle for Death," which he always called me.

He negotiated the sale of his company to the Bank of Nova Scotia in December 1987, continuing to manage Scotia-McLeod and died in 1996.

Bill and Patricia Buckley were destined to meet me again twenty years later when we were went cruising together with British Prime Minister Lady Margaret Thatcher and her chatty husband, Denis.

Enlightenment

It is easy to say but staggering to my reality, that the British Empire had handed back more than a couple of dozen countries during my time in Hong Kong in the 1960s!

Soon after we settled in Canada, by the end of that decade, in addition Eswatini, Yeaman, Mauritius and Nauru had also gone.

They were running out of countries, however, and disposed of only just over a dozen in the 1970s: Fiji, Tonga, United Arab Emirates, Bahrain, Qatar, Seychelles. Solomon Islands, Kiribati, St Lucia, St Vincent, Dominica, Tuvalu, Grenada and the Bahamas.

Bahamians Ivern and Elma Davis

Ivern Davis had a happy grin in his face! Why not? His personal story, as for many in that era, was the journey from slavery to independence.

It was 1973 in the Bahamas and we were there to celebrate their long-sought total freedom. With family and friend connections, it had become our regular vacation destination of choice. The black community had finally taken control. They had been freed as slaves only 130 years previously.

Ivern and *Elma Davis* were a good example of those decedents who became close friends, welcoming us to stay at their home in Nassau and visiting us in Canada.

Understandably, with their despicable colonial history, the white folks who decided to stay were under political stress and there were years of wrangling and infighting.

Curiously, the non-Bahamian born people who stayed, were labeled 'Belongers'. If they wished to remain, they had to prove their value to the new country, which of course led to years of frustrating negotiation and payment.

Eventually things settled down and they developed the self-trusting, functional society of today.

Elma Davis was Matron of the hospital and Ivern ran the country's Engineering and City Planning Department. He had engineering qualifications from Toronto and city planning from the University of British Columbia.

The tall Ivern was squash champion of the Caribbean Islands. At his personal squash court at his house, he would just non-chalantly stand in the middle of a court with me running around in vain for the ball.They were proud of their Bahamian heritage. In self-defence I told him Granny Sarah, on my mother's side, came from abjectly poor farm labourers. She was born in the 1880s into quasi-feudal, poor conditions. They were tied to the land and she got no schooling, laboured as a child in the fields, 'stone picking' for a penny a day.

My mother, luckily being a very bright kid, made it to college, meeting my father through business."You see," I explained defensively to my supremely self-confident friend Ivern, reclining by his large hilltop pool, drinking his wine, "My granny was literally a serf too, impoverished and totally controlled."

"There's a lot of difference," said Ivern in his quiet, balanced way. "My grandparents' mother and father were born actual, real slaves, *owned* by you guys. Slaves! Can you imagine that? You could do anything with us. Defile out women on demand. Beat us and buy and sell us at will. Even sell our babies. And after being 'freed' my families were then unemployed and still abjectly poor, begging for work until my Dad's generation. They were degraded and held virtually no civil rights."

I stuttered in response, "Well, you and I don't recognise relationships that way now. I deplore how terrible the British Empire was. But it's not on my doing or on my personal conscience, so let's just move on."

He grinned, cheerfully refilling my glass.

"Easy for us to say!" he concluded.

We were lifelong friends and Ivern and Elma enjoyed long and productive lives as popular local celebrities.

Anthropologist Margaret Mead

In June 1976, increasingly visible Vancouver hosted the United Nations Habitat Conference on Human Settlements, 'Habitat. A Conference on the Humanities'.

Dr Peter Oberlander, a nationally prominent city planner, and I were appointed joint chairs to organise the parallel public participation program. It was a lot of work but fun, particularly with regard the visiting celebrities.

I drew two very interesting guests to host, Americans *Margaret Mead* and *Buckminster Fuller.* I missed out on *Paolo Soleri* the renowned Italian architect, *Dame Barbara Ward,* the British intellectual and economist, and (fortunately) on *Mother Theresa,* the prominent social working nun from Calcutta, all of whom however met me briefly at various functions.

* * *

Both of my personally assigned guests were getting on in years.

Margaret Mead was a very self-important and dignified 'old lady' although only 75 years old. She was dramatically slow moving, leaning heavily on her thumb stick which she used as a prop, both theatrically and practically.

Aware of her celebrity, particularly as an anthropologist, she preached pending world doom, and fed cheerfully into the general public worries.

After showing her around, slowly, for a couple of days, I escorted her to her formal luncheon address when she held the audience spell-bound with her stories and predictions. She was quite a remarkable person.

She was a frequent media speaker during the 1960s and '70s. She had a PhD from Columbia, but her fame came from her published anthropological studies which publicised her racy personal relationships in the Samoan jungle as a young, energetic and inquisitive woman.

Margaret had hinted strongly that her academic investigation had involved her personally with her energetic, scantily clad male subjects. Her books sold well!

She was married three times, each ending in publicly titillating circumstances, had children and ended her years in a happy lesbian relationship. Now, no big deals but interesting in those times.

Geodesic Buckminster Fuller

"Call me Bucky," was slightly older but sprightly, a designer, hands-on engineer, prolific author and inventor. *Buckminster Fuller* dropped out of Harvard being disciplined twice for misbehaviour, excessive partying, and 'lack of industry'. Then having spent the First World War in the American Navy, designed and built lightweight housing.This led to architecture and geodesic domes. He became a famous academic with a slew of prestigious awards including a long delayed honorary degree from Harvard. My *Queen of England* no less presented him with her Royal Gold Medal for Architecture! He also collected one for Literature. He was president of Mensa International and obviously fairly bright!

His inventiveness led him to design and patent the dramatic architectural biosphere form, the Geodesic Dome, which was a central feature as the US Pavilion, at the recent Montreal Expo 67.

He was still an active, bouncy lecturer at Southern Illinois University. He laughed that he was "Getting over the hill", and that a student had recently asked him, "Weren't you once Buckminster Fuller?" He was just over 80, a very chatty, personable little guy, and a lot of fun.

It was an absolute pleasure to spend time with each of them, but thank heavens I did not draw Mother Theresa, with whom I would have had absolutely nothing in common. Religions have caused more trouble than they were worth, especially throughout the Empire.

* * *

The United Nations' celebrity of celebrities was *Maurice Strong*, the Canadian UN Ambassador. Whoever else was there, he was 'The Presence'. He had built an enviable aura around himself. By Habitat he was floating at an ethereal level.

A self-made and bustling little businessman he made a fortune in the Alberta oil industry and until 1966 had been president of the Power Corporation of Canada. He then launched himself into a career to save the world and became one of the first advocates for the environment and sustainable development.

As a diplomat he was appointed Under-Secretary General of the United Nations from 1972 to 1975, chairing the first Stockholm Conference on the Environment in 1972. By Vancouver Habitat in 1976 there was another conference secretary general, but he was still doyen of the environmentalists! He was whisked self-importantly from meeting to meeting delivering impressive missives with condemning direct eye contact.

I certainly made time available for him, but he settled for a brief chat and perfunctory handshake, before his fawning, protective entourage enveloped him and swept him away.

Premier Dr Michael Harcourt

But someone had noticed me. After the Habitat Conference, I was invited as a founder and executive member of the resultant International Centre for Sustainable Cities endowed at UBC in 1993. ICSC was chaired actively by *Hon. Dr Michael Harcourt.*

Mike had met me first, years before when he was a happy, hippy skinny lad with an Afro haircut. He ran a storefront law office, straight out of law school. He had filled out somewhat and controlled his hair. Now he was the dignified, left-leaning ex-Premier of British Columbia; the Honourable Dr Dr Dr … Mike Harcourt. He has about eight honorary doctorates which he jokes came from giving generous grants. He had resigned from the premiership very honourably but unnecessarily, taking the responsibility for a scandal not of his making.

Over the following years, we were involved in a series of programmes throughout the world, all conducting sustainable development, improving living conditions and starting as lowly as providing fresh water and cleaning up garbage! The Centre for Sustainable Development at Simon Fraser University still carries on the good work in a much more sophisticated style.

* * *

I had enjoyed my year back in the United Kingdom, in the mid-sixties, with the Grosvenor Estate. I had caught up with some of the British culture I had missed during my decade in Asia.

But by now I had switched to the North American way of life in

Canada with its media and television dominated by the neighbouring United States culture.

In the music world, the big event was Woodstock in New York State, which ended the 1960s dramatically with probably the most famous rock festival to that date. *Jimi Hendrix, Sly, The Who, The Grateful Dead, Janis Joplin, Creedence Clearwater* … all together in heavy rain and seas of mud.

But little did I know we were also entering years which would prove one of the worst decades for the industrialised nations since the Great Depression.

The early part of those seventies had started negatively with the disgrace of *President Nixon* through Watergate and the massacre at the Munich Olympics.

The Godfather and *Jaws* dominated the screens. *The Beatles* broke up in 1975 and the Vietnam War came to a bloody end. 'The King of Rock', *Elvis Presley*, died, an obese caricature of himself. *John Lennon* and *Yoko Ono* had moved to New York where he was shot to death. President Reagan was wounded in an assassination attempt.

Not the best of mixed times, but Canada generally went on developing steadily and quietly.

Actor Dudley Moore CBE

During our Canadian Freehold business days Stanley Kwok and I had the excuse of investments to visit 'tax deductively' throughout California.

We stayed at prestigious hotels in Hollywood and star watched. Many of the now-legendary Hollywood restaurants such as the Brown Derby and Chasens became our regular haunts. On an outdoor lunchtime patio Stanley ogled a noisy big central table.

"Look, *Angie Dickinson* and *Lee Majors*," he gasped.

They were TV stars of *Police Woman* and of *The Six Million Dollar Man*, appearing regularly on our home screens. Then someone at that star table jumped up, pointed in our direction and shouted, "Good heavens, can it be Stanley Kwok, the architect?"

"Man-Wai!" Stanley responded in great surprise. The blushing, perspiring Stanley was led to the central table and seated for a long lunch with all the stars. I ordered another bottle of white wine for myself, patiently observing the action until Stanley eventually brought Man-Wai back to our table.

It turned out he was the producer *Raymond Man-Wai Chow,* who had recently grown famous from making the incredibly successful martial arts Bruce Lee series. He started out studying engineering with Stanley at Shanghai University but later moved onto producing movies in Hong Kong.

There he had discovered *Bruce Lee* and personally risked everything in launching his career. But Bruce died suddenly, probably from 'over-stimulation' at the age of 32.

Fortunately, they had enough movies 'in the can' for Man-Wai to issue, and he profited enormously from Bruce Lee's sudden posthumous fame.

Years later, he capitalised on this background with the Jackie Chan movies. Stanley still talks about his lunch with the stars.

* * *

My personal moment came at the popular Century Plaza Hotel in central Los Angeles where I normally stayed at that time.

I was invited to a black-tie reception, and just turned casually towards a very familiar English voice.

A beautiful tall blonde was holding hands with the very talkative, short, but good-looking young fellow, whose head barely reached her eyeline.

That did not seem to bother him and why would it? British actor *Dudley Moore*, who then lived in Los Angeles, had recently released the smash hit move, *10* with *Bo Derek*. This chatty women with him, however, was his recent wife *Tuesday Weld.*

I was on my own and they accepted me into their informal group.

We were all shouting over the party din, no doubt making profound observations about the issues of the day, but Dudley had our rapt attention. He had a gift of personal engagement and a naturally funny way of expressing himself, while laughing happily at his own jokes.

A couple of years later he went on to act as an 'amusing' drunk in *Arthur*, another big hit, which won him an Oscar nomination.

However, his life evolved tragically when he announced he had a brain disorder, PSP, like Parkinson's disease. He died officially of pneumonia at the turn of the century.

Just before he died, when he was very frail, our Queen summoned him to Buckingham Palace, where he was appointed a Commander of the British Empire by Prince Charles.

Au, My Lord Georgeham

The Freehold Development company we had built so assiduously since 1970 was sold out from under us by the controlling shareholders in 1980. Not that we suffered financially. Interest rates internationally had spiked to a remarkable high, and it was a good time to sell.

The buying company Canadian Pacific Railway did not need the company name, so we continued as Freehold with our biggest project a 4500-acre housing estate in Calgary.

It had been agreed that China would take back Hong Kong in 1997 and a flow of old friends emigrated back into our lives. We were outbid on a deal by a mysterious person from overseas. Our competitors also shrugged that the crazy offshore offer was impossibly excessive.

A friendly banker laughed that it was a famous eccentric billionaire from Hong Kong called *Au Bak Ling.* I said, "There can only be one Au Bak Ling in the world."

I dug out and faxed him photos of two sweaty young men with arms around each other's shoulders drinking beer in a grubby Hong Kong Wanchai bar. But street bookseller Au Bak Ling, a billionaire?

It was indeed Bak Ling. A few months later he arrived to survey his new estate. We offered a local partnership, but he said he was a big boy. He never trusted anyone and owned his publishing empire entirely personally. So, he proceeded with his development, learning and losing money cheerfully, as he went.

Bak Ling had always been a stubborn fellow. We first met through business when I arrived in Hong Kong as a youngster. He had appalling general manners, spat out chewed meat at meals, a common Cantonese practice, hawked occasionally on the street and spoke aggressively, trying to stare down any opposition. But he was intelligent, friendly and under his brusque exterior very willing to learn.

Back then we sometimes had meals in Western-style restaurants so that he could learn to dine 'correctly'. He had been born on the street in Hong Kong, started work at eight and left school when he was ten.

He was brought up in abject poverty, barefoot and begging in the alleys. He had never continued education and was completely self-taught.

When Hong Kong fell to the Japanese in 1941 his father had disappeared amid famine, and he supported his entire family. He started his own little street stall business in 1943, called Ling Kee, reselling anything he could scrounge. When he met me, almost twenty years later, by sheer hard work and self-education he had transformed it into Ling Kee Book Stores.

I left Hong Kong and we had lost touch. Now he explained he had bought the overseas rights to Western and European textbooks and published them in Chinese and Asian languages selling to an enormous market. Hence, he said triumphantly, "I am way more than a dollar billionaire now."

His daughter, an accomplished pianist at the Juilliard School in New York, moved to Vancouver to manage their apartment buildings and the land development, but he appeared from time to time.

* * *

The last time I took him to my club for dinner in Vancouver I had a bit of fun with him by disputing whether he really was a billionaire. I asked him, "If you needed to give someone a million, what would you do?"

He replied confidently, "I would pull out my cheque book and write him a cheque, put a note in the margin and tell my accountant later."

"Would you miss the money?" I asked.

"Of course not," he said. "It would disappear into the rounding."

"Well," I said, "if you really are a billionaire, write me a million-dollar cheque. Or even better, since I'm a bit short this month, make it two million. Canadian dollars will do."Bak Ling spluttered in indignation that he would never cause his good friend to lose face by begging for money. No, he would not consider it. I said, "Ha! You're not really a billionaire."

Bak Ling just held my gaze in perplexity and shook his head. That was the last time we happened to meet before Au became a total recluse. Our friends said he had gone strange. He worked in isolation in his Hong Kong apartment directing his many companies and extensive charities.

He also insisting upon being addressed as My Lord of Georgeham, an English title he seemed to have purchased. I would have had much fun with him about that because he took himself so seriously.

* * *

Taking a traditional Chinese view, Stanley Kwok said I had put Bak Ling in a difficult position. "If he had started to write a cheque he could have made you lose face terribly. But he was very charitable person and by not doing so, he might have let down a good friend who really did need help."

Stanley asked. "And what would clever you have done if he had given you a couple of million bucks?"

"Good question," I replied. "I would likely have applied some sound Western logic, thanked him very much, put it in my pocket and confirmed he was a billionaire!"

Au might well have believed I was short of money because the 1970s had been terrible years for business in the Western world. He was aware some of my ex-colleagues in Hong Kong had driven their companies into near bankruptcy by over-extending.

Not a good start to the new decade and I had obviously not picked the best of times to move to North America.

Fortunately, the company I was running had been well financed and had little debt, so in many ways by having cash we benefitted from other people's difficulties. Au Bak Ling was not to know that, of course, but he was not forthcoming with the requested giveaway money, anyway!

* * *

My formal partnership with Stanley lasted a few more years. He joined a voluntary board to construct Vancouver's new sports stadium, which led to a directorship in Expo 86. We and our families have remained close friends.

Following Expo, he became the first ethnic Chinese in Canada appointed President of a Crown Corporation and proceeded to plan the redevelopment of the entire Exposition property. He believed the province should plan and rezone the site and sell it off in sections. After some years the political decision was made to put it on the market as a block and he resigned believing this was the wrong approach.

We had rejoined for a few months when, out of the blue, he was invited back to Hong Kong where for the first time he met *Mr Li Ka Shing*, their richest man.

Mr Li successfully bought the entire Expo site in an international competition and Stanley agreed to head up his development company in Canada.

He planned and managed the development of the prime 170-acre property, producing one of the most successful and livable, high-density, city centre urban areas in the world.

This is a widely recognised and outstanding achievement and Dr Stanley Kwok is known as a British Columbia Living Legend!

Lt Governor the Hon. David Lam

Just like Stanley, my friends *David* and *Dorothy Lam* left a very comfortable way of life in Hong Kong and arrived in Vancouver, to start again, a few months after me in 1967. Twenty years later, he was Lt Governor of British Columbia, Her Majesty the Queen's personal envoy.

* * *

The Lams had arrived with no fanfare, accompanied by their pretty little daughters and just with their suitcases, but by the late 1980s were making a fortune for themselves and his charities. They were also making history.

I knew them from Colonial Hong Kong, originally meeting when I organised the first Harvard Business School diploma course in the colony, from which we had both 'graduated'. Well, we got fancy diplomas! The Lams were already drifting around Hong Kong in chauffeur-driven limousines when I lived there and gave very impressive parties.

Then in the mid-1960s, Hong Kong suffered riots instigated by the Red Guards from over the border, starting local anticipation of the imminent Communist takeover from the British.

This was all leading to mounting insecurity and many people decided to relocate to more stable democracies.

Thus, Stanley Kwok and family had turned up in Vancouver. Then David and Dorothy with their young daughters, Deborah, Daphne and Doreen!

Stanley and I went to greet them where they stayed, initially in the West End of Vancouver, surprised that such a successful, very established traditionally Hong Kong entrepreneur would start up again in a new city.

David Lam was educated in Hong Kong and went on to Temple University in the US. His extremely wealthy family were in banking, coal and many businesses, among other things steel production. They had cleverly purchased surplus battleships around the world, towed them to Hong Kong and put them through enormous extrusion machines producing the reinforcing bars and steel in high demand.

David went back to school at the University of British Columbia to study real estate and invested readily available Asian money, making himself a fortune. He was a quietly spoken, very charming fellow and his calm wife Dorothy complemented him perfectly.

The Vancouver Club has a very racist history, and I encouraged my friends David Lam and Stanley Kwok to be among the first Chinese members as the club liberalised in the mid-1980s. I lunched there often with Stanley and one day David rushed over wide eyed in excitement.

He had been invited to be the first ethnic Chinese Lieutenant Governor of British Columbia. He said, in his typically modest manner, "Think Dorothy and I can do it?" Kidding him we said, "Well, at least Dorothy can!"

A few months later we attended their inauguration and the splendid be-medalled formal ball at Government House hosted by the beaming Hon. David and Dorothy.

* * *

Towards the end of the last century, I launched into the wholesale celebrity business as President of the Vancouver Canadian Club.

In connection with the club, I was appointed Chair of the Federal Citizenship Court in Vancouver, which was purely ceremonial but allowed me to make a pompous little speech welcoming new citizens.

There was a large influx of immigrants from Hong Kong and Lt Governor Hon. David Lam was famous to them. Mention of this wealthy, limo-riding son of Hong Kong always piqued their interest. This was followed as a good laugh and round of applause at my stated plight, the poor Gweilo still running in the rain for the bus, just like them.

David and Dorothy not only did the job with distinction but stayed in office from 1988 to 1995, one of the most beloved and cherished couples to receive that honour.

Chief Joe Mathias

The Squamish First Nation was assembled for ease of administration by the Federal Government from sixteen separate indigenous villages in 1923, and now controls valuable urban property. Their extensive holdings worth billions of dollars are surrounded by the city buildings but have remained stubbornly undeveloped mainly due to internal indecision and the restrictions of the Indian Act.

My first serious business dealings with the Squamish Nation were when I was Chair of the West Vancouver Planning Commission in the 1970s, particularly concerning their land and shopping centre land ownership at Park Royal.Their popular and revered leader was *Hereditary Chief Joe Mathias*, an apparently inexhaustible champion of native rights and vice-chair of the Assembly of First Nations. He was constantly in public and we had met briefly on several occasions, the last being at a Canadian Club lunch in March 1996, a few years before his early death at 56 in 2000.

The much more internationally famous local, *Chief Dan George,* never did get the opportunity to meet me, although I often saw him around. He had been Chief of the Tsleil-Waututh Nation, a Coastal Salish Band and after a long acting and television career in Canada, hit it big at the age of 70 in Hollywood. His crowning role was the movie *Little Big Man* with Dustin Hoffman. He was nominated for an Oscar as Supporting Actor of the Year.

In the 1980s the Squamish-elected Chief invited a group of us professional city people to join their development advisory committee. We helped their management team plan to deal with site pollution, create a deal and select an established development company, to build a sizeable shopping centre on some of their prime land by the Second Narrows Bridge. Most of our instruction came from the powerful Band Managers.

The Nation was to put the land in at market value for 99 years and the developer took the risk, provided the development cash and guaranteed financing. Band employment and training was to be assured during construction and for the life of the project. Training programs were started.

During the life of the mortgage the two parties were to share income in proportion to their investment and then the Band had a series of options to buy out the private developer at an agreed formula. Both the advisory committee and the Chief's management committee approved the project deal with enthusiasm.

Contracts were drawn up but not signed. The project never happened because the Nation itself after raucous meetings could not agree to proceed. The land was still vacant 30 years later and the jobs had not been created.

A young voting Band member told me later that they distrusted the advisory committee. "You are white guys, and you were obviously on the other side. The Chief and committee were in cahoots with you too, so we would have been silly to agree. Something was going on!"

Whatever the reasons, nothing happened,

* * *

Far away in Calgary during our Freehold Development days Stanley Kwok and I started developing Douglasdale Estates, a 4500 acre, 6500-home suburb in Calgary. In exchange for planning concessions, we agreed to convey our entire Bow River Valley frontage to the city for use as a public park.

A city prior requirement was that the hundreds of 'dangerous' beavers living on the riverbank be humanely trapped and transferred way down-river to new homes. They recommended I contact the Chief of a skilled Indigenous group way south of the city and I met him at the Douglasdale Golf Club bar.

"What we will do," he advised, "is employ dozens of our trappers luring the beavers by their favourite foods. Then, humanely transfer them way down south to our reserve and release them along the riverbank where they will be very happy in their new home."

His business-like contract reassured the City Parks Department. It was a slow, expensive process over many months, but the Parks Board certified a successful operation. Everyone was happy except, maybe, the beavers.

Some years later, but no longer involved with the project, I dropped into the golf club for a beer. There at the bar was the Chief together with a few of my old friends from the Band. After a long and pleasant chat plus several beers I asked, "How did the beavers all settle in, down south?"

The Chief moved closer and with a twinkle in his eye replied, "Beaver hats!"

* * *

Early in the new century, yet another Chief of a semi-rural Coastal Indigenous Band asked me for advice on industrial development on their land. *Chief Gary Feschuk* explained they had little commercial real estate experience and we got on very well for months planning the development of an industrial park together. They had centrally located land on the highway, and the Coast particularly needed modern warehousing.

It would require local road upgrades and servicing outlay offered by the Provincial Government, but initial meetings looked good, and I helped the Chief and Band council to draw up detailed plans, get construction quotes and submitted proposals.

Their argumentative and noisy meetings were usually at their Council office with a lot of dissension from the younger members, but occasionally it provided an excuse to meet at the Vancouver downtown Hotel Georgia.

The gentlemanly Chief Feschuk struggled to keep order!

The Band meeting dragged on all morning and finally one of the young Band members, wanting no doubt to get to the bar and lunch, said blandly, "We've heard enough, John. Why don't you just sod off!" He used somewhat stronger language!

The already frazzled Chief leaped to his feet in consternation and shouted, "Speak politely to John. He is our guest."

The young fellow rose slowly and to cheers from his young supporters, said in a friendly manner, "OK, John, why don't you *please* sod off!" I grinned. He had potential! It was all in a sense of fun and showed they were comfortable with me.

Finally, the industrial park was approved and the province would provide the servicing and entrance roads.

Inspecting the property, I was aghast, however, to find unplanned construction already underway across the essential industrial park service entrance.

At the Band Office, I found the defeated Chief shrugging that the younger members had decided to accept an offer and voted to build a gas station instead of constructing the large industrial park.

"It was an inside proposal and the guys decided to take the first deal which came along. They offered immediate jobs! Sorry about that, John. Thanks for your help!"

No beaver hats to sell, but probably good jobs pumping gas.

* * *

I was later again asked by an Indigenous group to help develop plans for the Squamishs' prime high-rise complex on downtown Burrard Street, but it was not until 2023 that serious plans were produced for a massive 11-tower, 6000-unit, rental development to be financed by the Federal Government.

They were finally getting into big business!

If only *Chief Joe Mathias* could be around now to see this. He would be about eighty and would have been the grand old gentleman of the Nations, seeing his dreams of indigenous reconciliation and financial independence beginning to come true.

* * *

Yes, Canada was changing progressively. I had already seen Montreal abdicate its premiere position as Canada's brilliant bilingual cultural and business centre, to the correct and dowdy unilingual Toronto.

Almost all the major companies with which I dealt had moved to Ontario taking me there for meetings, often monthly.

Vancouver and Calgary were both also developing quickly, reinforced by immigration in British Columbia, oil in Alberta and imported goods from the manufacturing powerhouse, Japan, plus increasingly from China.

In addition to the high interest rates and economic stress, the 1980s had opened in the depth of the Cold War due to United States and Russia being seriously engaged in the arms race. This was putting Europe under severe strain, particularly the still-separated East and West Germany. To add to the problems Iraq invaded Iran!

The United States had started its AIDS crisis.

Still, it was a blockbuster decade internationally for entertainment: *Top Gun*, *Sophie's Choice*, *Chariots of Fire*, *The Color Purple*, *The Shining* and *Gandhi* among the leading movies.

Pop and hip-hop were sweeping the globe. Video games had appeared, in arcades. The Walkman portable music devices arrived, together with ending the bulky boom boxes and the need for home stereo systems. Music was dominated by flashy stars such as *Madonna* with her *Like a Virgin*, *Bon Jovi, Duran Duran, Iron Maiden, Tears for Fears and Prince.*

Even back-water Canada was on the international scene with *Rush, The Tragically Hip* and *Loverboy*.

Flamboyant *Pierre Trudeau* was still in style and remained Canadian Prime Minister for more than fifteen years, retiring only after his decisive 'walk in the snow'. He had dramatically introduced the problematic Patriation of the Canadian Constitution in 1982 and was followed by Conservative *Brian Mulroney* who negotiated the vital US Canada Trade Agreement in 1988.

It was the sad time of *Terry Fox's* death from cancer during his brave cross-Canada Marathon of Hope run.

Nevertheless, the two-term *American President Reagan* finished the decade on a very high note when he joined with Russian *Mikhail Gorbachev* to bring down the Berlin Wall in November 1989, ending Communism in Europe, freeing Germany, Poland, Hungary and other controlled countries. This essentially ended the Cold War and the arms race, formally at least!

* * *

Still associated with Imperial Chemicals, I had found myself increasingly called to business meetings in the golfing paradise, British Bermuda. Then, later in the dull, once colonial, Delaware. ICI had registered companies in both places taking advantage of the expanding international 'off-shore' tax evasion systems, a sure sign of things to come.

Elevation

After its two decades of frantic disposal, in the 1980s the tired Empire had slowed to a trot. They were running out of countries to liberate but freedom had been granted to Antigua, Belize, St Kitts, Zimbabwe and Brunei.

Prime Minister Benazir Bhutto

Without any doubt the most tragic and beautiful celebrity to make my acquaintance was *Benazir Bhutto.*

When I first dropped into Karachi long before, on my 1958 voyage to Asia, Pakistan had only achieved its independence as a Muslim Dominion, from the Empire (and from India) a decade previously.

Then there was West and East Pakistan, in one physically divided country but Benazir's part, the western area, broke off as the separate country Pakistan, after a civil war in 1971.

Back in 1958, the docks and surrounding area at the noisy, grubby and seething port town of Karachi gave the impression of an agrarian country struggling towards industrialisation with much of the transportation still being pulled by hand or by their characteristic, noisy camels. Streets were dirty and the people mainly unkempt, although the clubs and hotels were typically grand and exclusively Colonial.

After the civil war, now with a population of more than 200 million, nuclear capability and the sixth largest army in the world, Benazir's Pakistan was a force to be reckoned with, especially by its neighbouring foe, India.

* * *

Prime Minister Benazir Bhutto entered dramatically, looking magnificent, with her small entourage, stylishly dressed in a long gown and wearing a token veil over her shining long hair.

We were in a quiet anteroom reserved for private pre-dinner cocktails. Nearby we could hear the Vancouver Hyatt Regency ballroom buzzing in anticipation. It was in 1991 and a black-tie World Affairs Society dinner event and charity fundraiser. I had been talked into a sponsorship, hence the privileged audience.

We had been warned to move off to join our tables promptly, but stayed on when we saw that she was politely trying to get around greeting everyone.

She did not shake hands but make direct contact with each person, connecting personally with her large serious brown eyes and chatting gently for a few moments.

Contrary to a previous guest speaker, *Rev. Jesse Jackson*, the American activist and Senator, a tall, powerfully built ex-football player, who seemed intent upon breaking every bone in my hand.

Benazir's reputation preceded her, but she was a poised and striking young woman at the time only 38. She was of course not as innocent as she appeared!

What she had packed into her life to that point was remarkable. She was born in Pakistan in 1953 to a wealthy political family. Her somewhat socialist father Zulfikar was elected Prime Minister of Pakistan in 1973, inciting a right-wing military coup led by General Mohammad Zia. Her father was deposed, imprisoned and executed in 1977. Not a helpful start to her political career; or good for his, of course.

She had been getting herself impressively educated at Harvard and Oxford earning three degrees, arriving back in Pakistan just in time for her father's downfall. She became an outspoken political nuisance and was imprisoned herself several times leading to her exile to the UK in 1984.

A couple of years later she was allowed to return for an arranged and political marriage to a wealthy businessman, Asif Zardari. She could not resist politics however, but conveniently her arch enemy President Zia was killed in a mysterious plane crash.

Elected Prime Minister of the turbulent Pakistan at the age of 35 in

1988, she was the first female leader of a major Muslim country. "Too young to be Prime Minister," many critics complained in Pakistan, to which President Khan had added, "And corrupt!", meaning not sharing the proceeds of corruption. He used that as his reason to force the end of her rule 'constitutionally' after only two years.

She set out on her world speaking tour, stating her case very eloquently as expected of a past president of the Oxford University Union. Obviously, she was a controversial figure dangerously poised between the modern world and traditional Muslim beliefs.

I was totally captivated by the very self-assured but charming and attractive young woman. There was nothing about her of the solid and domineering Maggie Thatcher whom she so admired.

* * *

She was obviously not a quitter and after she had met me, she returned to Pakistan, raised three children and got herself re-elected prime minister from 1993-96. She continued as leader of her Pakistan Peoples' Party all her life.Pakistan is one of the most corrupt countries in the world, so mutual charges of corruption among the power group are meaningless. However, Benazir and her husband Asif later found themselves hounded by such claims, imprisoned, exiled and suffering all the usual vile Pakistani political manoeuvrings over the following decade.

* * *

Years later in 2007 I was driving home from the office through Stanley Park when I heard the radio news Benazir had been assassinated. She was working on yet another election campaign and while speaking in public had been shot and killed.

The personal memory of that bright young woman with so much still to offer, brought tears to my eyes. Like me, she too, had been a Child of the Empire.

Paul McCartney

Since I came to Canada my life had been concentrated in North America, the Caribbean and to a limited degree Asia, but twenty years later business and circumstances drew me back again frequently and for periods of time to the United Kingdom and Europe.

Immediately recognisable, *Paul McCartney* wandered into the lounge in the South of England, poured himself a coffee, and said, "Hello".

Already approaching 50 and long before he became Sir Paul,

(or 'When I'm 64!') he already looked mature. We were just two middle-aged guys meeting up in a spacious charming old private countryside hospital, worried about family health problems.

Young members of our families who knew each other well, were off in another part of the room chatting animatedly.

We briefly discussed the usual social things English fellows do and appreciated the splendid private medical facilities. Music, or attainment never intruded, we had more important personal family issues on our minds.

Years before, demonstrating Hong Kong's growing image as an international tourist centre, in the summer of 1964 *The Beatles* arrived in Asia. We attended their concert at the Princess Theatre on Nathan Road where they fought a losing battle with the constant organised screaming.

We acknowledged each other in the hospital from time to time over the passing months, but I never did get to call him Paul.

* * *

However, on another visit to England, I did have the pleasure of taking to dinner, probably the second most famous woman in the country at that time, after my Queen of course!

We dined in a smart Soho restaurant and the attention 'we' got was remarkable. The *maître d'* and waiters competed to serve us, and the rest of the patrons paraded by, gapping in interest.

I had realised just how famous she was, while travelling up to London first class by train in the morning. An unbroken business rule was to hide behind the *Financial Times* or *Economist* and never engage in conversation. That morning, however, I mentioned to my business companion that *Erika Roe* was my niece and every one of the newspapers went down sharply to listen. Soon the compartment was a buzz of excited comment.

Much later my wife and I came across *Erika* dignified prominently in the National Portrait Gallery, just head and shoulders!

So, why all the attention to my pretty little niece, whom I had first met in central Africa at her family tea plantation when she was a lusty three-year-old in the sun on a blanket.

Erika is renowned as the first female stripper to excite Twickenham Stadium, when at halftime of the game between England and Australia in 1982, she impulsively decided to take off her top and run across the pitch to the delight of the enormous crowd and the international television audience.

She is very attractive and well endowed, plus confidently spoken, so she very naturally immediately became a national phenomenon and celebrity.

After all the attention and fuss she retired off to Portugal to lead a sensible, quieter life.

Celebrity wives

Louis Armstrong, the famous American jazz musician, had remarkably replaced Paul McCartney and the Beatles early in the 1960s at the top of the world charts with his *Hello Dolly*, which he mostly sang, with his distinctive, gravelly voice

Louis brought his band to Hong Kong on a concert tour in 1965 and we sat just a few rows from the famous trumpeter. He was only 64 but his trumpeting lip was apparently giving out and he sang rather a lot. However, it was a magical performance and of course he was extremely famous.

In the 1970s we were visiting a Bay Street shop in the Nassau where a relative of ours was helping.

Louis had died in 1971 and his wife *Lucille Armstrong*, still a celebrity herself in New York, visited the Bahamas regularly.

She appeared to be well known in the shop chatting to us all in a friendly way. She had been a professional dancer at the Cotton Club in Harlem when she met Louis in 1939 and they had married in 1942. She was unaffected, personable and very friendly.

* * *

An entirely different wife, but just as well known internationally, lived a few miles away and enjoyed the Caribbean atmosphere of Bay Street, although she probably never met Lucille Armstrong. She was *Lady Eunice Oakes.*

She had met me socially in Nassau and we had the pleasure of entertaining her in Hong Kong when she passed through on a trip back to her original Australia.

She arrived at our modest home for lunch splendidly dressed and fully jewelled, causing me to scurry away to find a jacket.

But she was, after all, basically an Aussie and not withstanding her remarkable experiences in life, was very down to earth.

News of the bizarre, still unsolved, ritual murder of her husband, Canadian gold multi-millionaire Sir Harry Oakes in the Bahamas in 1941 had stunned the world.

Remarkably, this had mysteriously happened while the abdicated, ex-King of England was the governor of the colony, cozied up to his controversial wife, *Mrs Simpson.* And making a total mess of the murder investigation.Harry Oakes' son-in-law Alfred de Margay, who was married to his daughter Nancy, had been charged with the murder but was brilliantly defended to acquittal by local barristers *Godfrey Higgs* and *Ernest Callender,* who still sat amiably drinking beer most weekends in the upstairs bar of the Sailing Club. Their families have remained our life-long friends.The Oakes family continued to live in the Bahamas and joined regularly in local social events.

On one occasion *Lady Eunice* invited us to dinner at her palatial waterfront home. We arrived at her sweeping front entrance in our beat-up little dune beach buggy to the amusement of the liveried, white-gloved, tall butler assigned to park the cars. He squeezed into the driving seat with a roll of his eyes and roared away.

We should have borrowed my father-in-law's swanky Rolls, except only he was allowed to drive it. This was still in the days of a colonial life and "over the hill" shantytown living for a large proportion of the population. Times were about to change!

* * *

Another renowned wife (and daughter) *Baroness Mary Soames* made my acquaintance when we invited her to Vancouver to be the speaker at a Sir Winston Churchill Society dinner in 1979.

She kindly signed her latest voluminous book which celebrates the long, long life of her mother Clementine Churchill.

We were somewhat privileged because her husband, the politician *Baron Christopher Soames,* had only been elevated the previous year, creating her Baroness Soames. (Oh no, not another 'Lady!' Mind you, the fact that she was Winston Churchill's daughter was far more elevating and interesting.)

Being on the Society board gave us the opportunity of spending a day or two entertaining our fascinating visiting speakers at that time emerging from the Empire era. As plain Mary Soames, she had served in the Territorial Service during The War and still retained a friendly standard conversational style. Nevertheless, we were all guarded in what we said, overawed by presence the Great Man's daughter. The War was still very much a part of our psyche.

Prime Minister Maggie Thatcher

The Hon.Margaret Thatcher didn't quite ask me to call her Maggie and at that point, anyway, she was not quite yet Baroness Thatcher. But we discovered her husband, the friendly *Denis Thatcher*, in the background and we went off to chat about cricket!

My close friend and colleague *Robin Cordwell* had kindly included me on a short fun jaunt aboard the recently launched *Regal Princess* through his P&O Shipping connection, sailing out of New York at the beginning of August 1991. Only our select group of invitees were on the first short cruise, in first class of course, led by the guests of honour *Sir Denis* and *Lady Margaret Thatcher.*

Neither Robin nor I was married at the time, so we went together, chaperoned by his pretty daughter.

The star celebrity aboard was of course Margaret Thatcher, but just along to enjoy herself; no pompous speeches just a relaxed brief friends-among-friends ship 'launching' presentation in the morning.

Recently, in November 1990, Margaret Thatcher had been forced to resign as Prime Minister after eleven tumultuous years during which she had survived an actual bombing attempt. She must have upset someone.

Now she was just a lowly Member of Parliament, although you would not have thought so!

* * *

And here we all were having a jolly cruise together!

She seemed relaxed, chatting amiably with anyone near her, although she made direct eye contact in a somewhat challenging way and spoke in her cultivated stentorian tones.We all had a chance to move close for brief encounters, but she was mostly enveloped in the official group led by *Lord Jeffrey Sterling* the P&O chairman. Denis on the other hand seemed to be happy to gravitate to the bar and just chat with us all in a highly amiable fashion.

Years before, I met a woman who had studied with Margaret Thatcher at Somerville College in Oxford and went to elocution lessons with her. That story obviously made me biased, but I had always thought her accent rather forced and phoney. Denis on the other hand sounded like one of the lads! But she was the one that made it to Prime Minister!

The little voyage was a wonderful example of the wheels within wheels of politics and commerce. Jeffrey Sterling had started out as plain grammar school boy, just like me, but in Reigate Grammar. Similarly, Maggie Thatcher began at the lowly Grantham Girls School. There the similarities end!

Jeffrey went on to do well financially as a stockbroker, making a lot of money and getting control of P&O Shipping among other things.

He had been knighted *Sir Jeffrey Sterling* in 1985. He was always an avid Thatcher supporter, and generous party contributor and he was further elevated in the Thatcher resignation honours list in December 1990 a few months before this voyage. He was now *My Lord Sterling*, entertaining the previous Prime Minister to a thank you voyage on one of his ships.

The next year in 1992 she resigned from the Commons and moved on to join him in the House of Lords as Baroness Thatcher of Kesteven.

The Billionaire Reichmans

There were other invited celebrities along on that star-studded cruise that had made my acquaintance previously.

William Buckley Jnr and *Patricia Buckley* happened to line up next to us as we all staggered from the generous opening cocktail party into the dining room. Yes, even celebrities line up on occasion, but only with fellow celebrities! Our previous meeting took a little explanation, but the light of their memory dawned. The Buckleys were soon chatting, if not like old friends, maybe as vague acquaintances. Later, they at least nodded in passing!

* * *

The other 'friends' I boasted to Robin about, were fellow Canadians *Paul* and *Albert Reichman* of Olympia and York, owners of the world's largest real estate empire.

Paul had once wandered into my Vancouver office unannounced

to try to buy one of our properties. He preferred never to use brokers, to save fees. We negotiated personally for months but never settled on a price.

Now they were stuck with us, being seated at the same table. At dinner, we sailed majestically down the Hudson River, pausing at the Statue of Liberty. We steamed past the downtown office area in the evening gloom. Emboldened by the liberal table wine, we joked tactlessly with the Reichmans that all their city office buildings were dark.

They responded with politely managed, stained smiles. The 1991 high interest recession had hit and it was common knowledge in the business world that their New York empire and Canary Warf in London had many vacancies and financial problems.

It turned out our innocent attempt at humour was rather cruel. O&Y filed for an enormous, highly publicised bankruptcy the following year in May 1992, only nine months after the cruise, owing some twenty billion dollars.

No doubt some interesting conversations went on in Margaret Thatcher's ultra-private luxury suite! She had disastrously invited the Reichmans to London to develop Canary Wharf following their early success at the World Financial Centre in New York and they had taken over its development in 1988.

Her long-promised Jubilee Line extension had not yet happened, and the banks would not relocate offices. Then the market had slumped and interest rates had gone crazy and they were broke, including their American assets! O&Y declared bankruptcy May 1992.

But Lord Sterling's ships sailed on confidently and Maggie had her peerage.

* * *

The century was moving to a close, I would be 65 years old and the unexpected just went on happening!

When I arrived in Hong Kong in 1958, we had progressed beyond Morse Code, and we had international telephone cables connecting us to the world. Although expensive, immediate communication around the world was possible.

However, anything in writing was sent by mail, cable or transposed, and long documentation was pricey and complicated. Our Hong Kong office accepted a couple of months as normal mail turnaround time.

In 1960 I remember sitting in the Cricket Club at lunch, aghast at a friend who had announced he had given up a solid local job to become the Asian representative for a new company called weirdly, Xerox. We all laughed at him.

But it was the beginning of the hi-tech revolution and of course he was on to a good thing and retired young! We just could not believe that a machine in the corner of the office could send, receive and spew out complicated printed documents immediately and on demand. Twenty-four hours a day!

The same type of revolution applied to calculators. At the time, in Hong Kong, our general office staff all used the abacus. The loud click clack sounded all day long.

I proudly had an almost silent, super-modern, hand-operated mechanical calculator with figure levers to be set and a handle at the side to wind for addition or subtraction, backwards or forwards. My guys were way faster on their abacus, but on my machine, you could see the figures. The abacus just produced a result.

By the time I left Hong Kong ten years later, our calculators had become electrically driven and with practical keyboards. The little wooden abacus was still faster and very much cheaper!

* * *

In the early 1970s, now in Canada, I was invited to the first North American symposium on the possible application of computer technology to real estate analysis. Possible application!

This was held at a university and the equipment was still in development. The massive computer was housed in a sealed glass room and operated by academics wearing green protection gowns!

Xerox meantime had expanded into one of the most successful international communication systems and my rich friend had fortunately long retired, because they were overtaken and wiped out by better technology.

Then everything all started moving fast.

In June 1970, the Windows system arrived, improving data-processing communication. Email came in 1971; then video games and mobile phones; 1973 digital cameras; 1975 the first commercial video games and microprocessors. Datapoint 200 provided the first modern type keyboard and screen.

In the 1980s and '90s internal restricted email was used by some advanced companies and by the military and universities. Then, in the mid-'90s the public were using it.

The first email network had developed in North America in 1971, but was not used commercially until the 1980s.

My company started employing computer technology in the early 1990s when I received my first desk computer and attended an explanation seminar.

We knew vaguely what a cell phone was, but they were not generally used, due to lack of networks. No one yet knew what 'AI' stood for.

* * *

Still. It was not all heavy stuff! My life too had taken a change, as I was between marriages, and my sons *Bob* and *Paul* had rock bands which exposed me, unexpectedly, to the Vancouver nightlife: Rymes with Orange (sic) and Mushroom Trail.

The other Canadian national bands came up with names like The Tragically Hip and The Barenaked Ladies. Internationally, in my new musical interest, I learned to expect bands such as Nirvana, Pearl Jam, Red Hot Chili Peppers, The Smashing Pumpkins and Alice in Chains!

It was a helpful diversion, but as the century drew to a busy close, I was very active in business and travelling extensively, particularly in the United States.

The Cambridge University English scientists *Drs James Watson* and *Francis Crick* became super celebrities with their DNA discoveries, leaving poor *Dr Rosalind Franklin*, who did much of the spade work, in their scientific dust.

Nelson Mandela who had spent 27 years in prison on political charges, shone as his country's balanced and unifying president.

The closing trial of the century was held in the United States, when football star *OJ Simpson* was charged with the bloody murder of his wife *Nicole Brown* in a dramatically televised show performance. This exposed affairs among the lawyers, celebrity posturing and extended fixing of evidence by the local police. OJ was of course acquitted.

I happen to have influenza and spent a few days in bed watching the court performance and ended convinced, on the contrived evidence as presented, that not guilty was the right verdict, even if he, in fact, did it!

A further entertaining spectacle was provided by the admittedly two-term American *President Bill Clinton*, who survived his impeachment involving some hanky-panky with an intern in the White House basement. He claimed "not to have sex with that woman", which appears to be technically possible since he had left his evidence for posterity and DNA analysis externally on the summer dress she retained with pride. Somewhat different presidential standards from Mr Mandela.

The rogue *Saddam Hussein* of Iraq attacked Kuwait for its oil and other assets before being beaten back by the allies in the Gulf War. My friend and colleague *Major General Scott Eichl* was in charge of the Canadian Air Force in that skirmish and dined out for years on his war stories.

An obscure Islamic cleric called *Osama bin Laden* issued a fatwa condemning the United States to a jihad, holy war. No one in North America took him seriously. What could he do against the might of America?

And so my century ended.

Princess Diana

Without any doubt, the death which shocked the world at the end of that decade and century, was that of *Princess Diana*, in Paris on August 31, 1997. She was highly respected in Canada, which she had visited several times. It was tragic news.

I never had the pleasure of being in her company, but I did see her during the opening of Expo, and had a guarded account of her personally from my partner's wife, *Mim Kwok,* whom Princess Diana had befriended.

My partner Stanley Kwok had been appointed a director of Expo 86 in Vancouver and in May 1986 he and his wife accompanied *Prince Charles* and *Princess Diana* on the Royal Yacht *Britannia* from Victoria British Columbia to the opening of Expo.

Diana had chatted with Mim at previous briefings. Mim was delighted when she was sought out personally and taken by Diana for coffee alone with her, in her private Royal Suite, during the two-hour cruise back to Vancouver, sheltering also from the unseasonably cold May weather.

Mim was a very charming, sympathetic person and she listened quietly while the troubled Diana unburdened herself quite freely about her life and personal struggles. Mim said Diana was a very distressed young woman and just clearly wanted someone to whom to talk and escape from all the dignitaries on board. Otherwise, Mim was very discrete.

Diana appeared to be unwell during that trip and while attending Expo suffered a dramatic fainting spell at one point, officially brought on by an eating disorder.

It is clear in retrospect her relationship with Prince Charles had understandably failed, if it ever started, and the world is fully aware of the eventual tragic consequences.

Princess Diana's premature death and the conveyance of my Hong Kong Colony to Communist China both in 1997 ended a century of dramatic change. Almost all the countries of my heritage were gone.

The Child of the Empire was bereft!

Fulfilment

Rather neatly, having relinquished Hong Kong in 1997, the Empire had fulfilled its undertaking and closed itself down as the new century opened.

The British still held a dozen or so properties scattered around the world. But the Falkland Islands, for example, after a serious skirmish with Argentina, voted almost unanimously to remain British. Other territories showed no haste to leave.

The independent Commonwealth of Nations had gone from strength to strength, interestingly showing little acrimony and providing the economic union and mutual support intended for the freed countries of the Empire.

Colonialist VP George Clinton

The new century opened dramatically with the tragic terrorist attacks on New York and Washinton DC.

9/11 achieved notorious significance!

Being in Vancouver, on the West Coast, and three hours behind, we awoke to news of the ongoing dramatic events at their outset and witnessed the trauma unfolding all day. I watched it all evolve with sadness. I had come to know New York very well.

* * *

New York State's *Vice President George Clinton* had also started out, a long time ago, as a Child of the Empire. Two-and-a-half centuries earlier. I learned George was born in Little Britain, New Jersey in 1739 and like me studied law, was a surveyor and did his military service. I immediate felt a kinship.

I had discovered him as I explored the United States for the first time back in the sixties.

His home had been New York, which was to become one of my favourite cities.

I had come up to town by train from Philadelphia, another early Empire trouble-making state, arriving at Penn Station, with just the need to fight my way across Seventh Avenue to the George Clinton Hotel.

There I discovered, ironically, that George was the first governor of the so-called freed New York State and instrumental in setting up the rebelling United States itself. He was not related to President Clinton, renowned for his incomplete sexual activity.

* * *

Way back on my first trip across America, I had headed eagerly towards New York for the first time, intent upon seeing yet another of my Queen's ex-territories, with a similar colonial history to the other states I was visiting.

But Britain had only acquired New York as late as 1664, when our fleet arrived and simply took it away from the Dutch.We had reluctantly soon given it up again due to George and those 1776 American colonial upsets, although the New Yorkers did not initially want to join the rebellion and held out for a year. Then it eventually becoming New York State itself.

* * *

George, however, was to become an Empire breakaway … Vice President of the rebelling United States. In 1776 he was appointed a brigadier general of the rebelling militia and he went downhill from then on, becoming Governor of New York State and eventually Vice President of the fledgling United States of America. At least he had started out well.

* * *

I was sadly witnessing our lost American Empire along my trip. The British made a half-hearted attempt at getting New York back later in the war of 1812 but after we had burnt down the White House, we decided it was not worth the effort. We were anyway extremely busy raiding other countries building up the rest of Empire.

I enjoyed my first stroll down Fifth Avenue, gazing up in awe at the skyscrapers, clambered up inside the Statue of Liberty, elevatored up the (then impressive) eighty floors of the Empire State Building, tramped around Grand Central Park, dutifully visiting The Met and The Guggenheim, and attended a concert at Carnegie Hall.

My light tourist and business presentation to the Junior Chamber of Commerce went well but the audience found my whole concept of the Empire and their past colonial life, well, ancient.

* * *

9/11! That title alone has become enough to mark September 11, 2001, as a date in infamy when New York received that most grievous terrorist assault.

The appalling, remarkable facts of the hijacked plane attacks on New York and Washington are well known.

It took eight months just to clear up the debris, then to 2006 to design and start building the replacement. It was November 2014 before everything was opened again.

As soon as we were able, we returned to the site, particularly to express our condolences, respecting the nearly three thousand people who were killed, at the splendid National September 11 Memorial and Museum.

It was ten years after the attacks when America caught up with and killed the instigator, *Osama Bin Laden* in Abbottsbad, Pakistan.

The attack on New York was a double whammy for business, which had opened the century during a market meltdown. Wall Street and the Stock Exchange are walking distance from the World Trade Centre and business was directly affected by the tragedy.

The new century had seen the initial collapse of the hi-tech market in March 2000. Two years later NASDAQ had lost 80 per cent of its value! The feared hi-tech bubble caused by speculative overpriced start-ups had been inflating since the middle of the 1990s and burst dramatically.

To add to the drama, the Paris-to-New York supersonic Concorde crashed on takeoff leaving Paris in July killing all on board. It was taken out of service the following year. I had been on a promotion tour of the plane at Heathrow, but was never on a flight. Such were New York's drastic opening two years of the century. Then a manned American space shuttle broke up on re-entry!

Those early years of the century were not all gloom and doom. Sydney hosted a summer Olympics. George Bush was elected in

America and Vladimir Putin in Russia. At least they were looked upon as positive at the time. The NASA Rover landed on Mars exciting future space speculation.

But overall, in North America, it was a dismal start to the century.

Adventurer Tony Buckingham

However, in July 2001, I was in the sun, enjoying a society wedding in celebrity country, Malibu, Los Angeles. Vancouver and the West Coast is a long way from New York and all the drama.

California is a warm attraction within easy travel distance of British Columbia and fortunately my business connections there have always necessitated regular visits. Several close friendships developed.

We were all casually, smartly dressed for the society garden wedding of prominent real estate developer *John Kilroy* to *Catherine* in the rolling celebrity-packed Malibu hills.

Celebrity-packed? For example, one evening I was dining in Malibu with John Kilroy, when he threw a bread roll across the room at another table.

A burley security guy came to our table and said politely, "Mr Carson would appreciate it if you would stop throwing buns at his table, please Mr Kilroy." The ageing *Johnny Carson* at the time lived on the same waterfront road as John and he waved cheerfully and came by later to say good night. They seemed to be well acquainted.

Another time with John late in the evening in a bar, we joined another couple, the lady apparently having dated him in high school. It turned out her friendly husband was *David Foster*, a fellow Canadian, pianist, composer and well-known producer, now settled in Los Angeles. We had a few beers and chatted mainly about Canada while John and his wife caught up on schoolmates.

Celebrities do apparently live day-to-day lives.

John Kilroy had divorced and sold his previous clifftop sea-view house, near Johnny Carson, to actress *Barbra Streisand* and the wedding was in the grounds of his grand new mansion set in extensive, manicured gardens.

I had been briefed by John that my dinner companion, an international sailing competitor of his, was 'a white mercenary from Africa', heavily involved particularly in the private supply of all types of combat aircraft including fighter jets through his Ibis Air company.

Whatever the truth, eyes had been rolled in his direction with a *sotto voce*, 'Executive Outcomes' which was the umbrella name of the mercenary activities with which he had been involved.

Tony Buckingham and his charming wife sat next to me, and we were quickly into an animated conversation.

They had my rapt attention with a series of fascinating tales. He explained that by the early 1990s, the bloody apartheid repression by de Klerk's South African white government, was being forced to an end. Mandela had been released and the deadly covert South Africa special military forces, a hangover from the oppressive Empire, were being disbanded.

They were essentially rehired by their former *Lt Colonel, Eeben Barlow,* and set up as a private mercenary group, the notorious Executive Outcomes, for covert actions especially in Angola, Sierra Leone (diamonds!) and throughout Africa, supporting the mercenary dictators emerging in the freed colonies.

This was clearly a well-connected and involved pair and as the wedding festivities ended, I was delighted we arranged to meet for breakfast to finish some of the engrossing stories of darkest Africa.

* * *

That decade of adventure during the 1990s in South Africa had consumed Tony, who was then not yet fifty, but I found he was already playing down his adventurous past.

He had now turned his attention totally to the oil industry having just the previous year, incorporated Heritage Oil on the Toronto Stock Exchange.

Both he and John Kilroy were prestigious international maxi sailors which accounted for their friendship.

The wedding was at the turn of the century and since that time Tony has joined the billionaire class and made a great success of Heritage Oil Corporation which he listed on the London Stock Exchange in 2008.

He has long claimed to have had no involvement, with those mercenary organisations since 1998 when he started running Heritage, but he has continued to be a highly controversial, newsworthy and intriguing personality.

'Adventurer turned oil baron' hardly does him justice!

Lord Jeffrey Sterling

Towards the end of the previous century developer *Robin Cordwell* had bought the Douglasdale Estate's 4500-acre housing project in Calgary I had been developing for years, for Sterling's P&O company, and the Lord himself came to Canada for inspection.

He arrived grandly in his personal jet at Alberta Airport, to be serenaded by Dougie our furry North American style uniformed mascot, which did not seem to amuse him particularly.

But he was impressed by the housing project, and we had a chatty dinner back at the hotel. Despite piercing eyes and a reserved nature, he was very affable and we enjoyed a wide-ranging conversation.

I just received a polite smile when I mentioned working for Jardine in Hong Kong. And that his P&O had been their drug-smuggling rival in Asia during the Opium Wars.

The next day he did not appear at breakfast, going straight back to his plane. His pilots joined us, however, and asked with a laugh whether anyone had checked his room.

Apparently, His Lordship dressed for the day and then walked out assuming someone would tidy up and pack his bag.

A few years later the relentless British tabloids had a field day when he was detained for allegedly not paying for his daily first-class commuter train ticket. No doubt he assumed someone had bought it for him and he just travelled every day without a thought!

***

Jeffrey Sterling is an almost exact contemporary of mine. He is just a few months younger than me and progressed from a grammar school background. As previously accounted, we met in business life, but although we had mutual friends at London University, I never met him there. He was into music then, but quickly went on into stockbroking and founded his own highly successful, Sterling Guarantee Trust.

He was offered a seat on the big establishment, P&O Steam Navigation Company's board in 1980 and quickly parlayed that into the commanding chairmanship by1983.

He used his new prestige and financial power to great personal advantage. He chose incredibly well to support Margaret Thatcher politically and financially, as previously recounted, and she kindly made him a Peer of the Realm.

He held on to the P&O chairmanship until 2005 when the *Telegraph* newspaper reported his pension plan was worth nine million pounds. But he was far from done. He was appointed President for Life of the P&O Cruise Lines.

Later, he became the highly prestigious National Chairman of the Queen Elizabeth Golden Jubilee Celebrations marking the Queen's 50th anniversary in 2010.He has always been outspoken and very newsworthy, exciting the tabloids, who once reported gleefully that he had suggested his cruise passengers embarking on the Swan Hellenic Line should not mix with other 'ordinary' ferry passages who were "mainly semi-lager louts or lorry drivers smelling of B.O."

Lord Sterling is still sitting and debating laws in the House of Lords, which is a life appointment. In 2020, this time using the most articulate and polished of prose, he delivered a beautifully crafted and heartfelt personal appreciation of our recently deceased monarch, Queen Elizabeth.

In all, not a bad performance for a grammar school boy!

Financier Norman Freeman

Imperial Chemical Industries and the Empire once had it made!

IG Fabin supplied Germany, Dupont the United States and ICI supplied the rest of the world.

Britain had 'ruled the waves' controlling the shipping routes. They had monopolised their markets, just took any raw materials they needed and manufactured everything without competition.Imperial Chemical Industries took maximum advantage of the situation and developed as Britain's biggest industrial group, producing general chemicals, plastics, paints, pharmaceuticals, explosives and much more to service the Empire.

The company became supreme when in 1926 Britain's four leading chemical companies had merged and set up a gigantic head office at Milbank London. At one point they employed 130,000 people in their endeavours.

The Second World War had finally broken up their monopoly as international competition grew. ICI was too big, was trying to do too many things and had become unmanageable.

When I came to Canada, ICI still appeared all powerful and their subsidiaries still dominated the markets throughout the Empire. Canada's largest chemical company was their subsidiary, Canadian Industries Limited, the controlling shareholder in my real estate company, Canadian Freehold.

That was when the flamboyant international financier *Norman Freeman* had the pleasure of commanding my presence at Millbank in London. I persuaded him to purchase a 20 per cent interest in Freehold and we started a long personal association.

At that time, pension funds throughout the world had not recognised the bond-like characteristics of prime real estate investment. Norman had successfully plunged into that market with the ICI Pension Fund, one of the largest in the world. He had met me on the international real estate speaking circuit where he was promoting his confidence in real estate.

In the present day, pension funds throughout the world hold substantial assets in prime real estate. In fact, it is a positive characteristic of Canada that our significant real estate is substantially institutionally owned with minimal debt.

It was typical of Norman Freeman personally that he had taken the plunge into real estate. He was not a prudent pension fund manager in the classic sense. He was flamboyant and one might say flexible.

For example, he and his colleagues at the pension fund, prominent 'London men about town', my friends *Tom Heyes* and *Bill Dobbie*, personally owned and ran a wild gambling night club on Swallow Street, just off Piccadilly, which considerably brightened my regular business visits to London.Norman eventually overstepped the mark with his private interests and was replaced by a dour, eccentric fellow called Alwyn Conlong, who had come from the Church of England Pension Fund and was absolutely no fun at all.

Alwyn became characterised by his eccentricities. He once flew first class from London to attend my board meeting in Calgary with leading Canadian businessmen wearing his ski outfit, complete with a comical ski hat. My board members were all decked out, of course, in their business suits. His explanation was that he travelled light and was going on to Banff.When he retired, and Tom Heyes took over as manager of the world's leading pension fund, he found Alwyn's desk drawers to be packed with cookies he had for years taken daily from the tea trolley and stored.

Tom was a brilliant fellow, who had been at London School of Economics with me, and he took to running the massive investment fund obsessively with his usual high energy. He and his wife Jean were close friends of mine and she tells the tale of his final weekend with a wan smile.

They were at a top-level financial conference, and he worked off his usual heavy hangover with an early morning game of squash and bacon-and-eggs breakfast, to read the financial news. Then onto more meetings and a business lunch with several pre-drinks and then a bottle of wine.

They had the afternoon free and retired to their suite for a couple of hours in bed. She left him asleep and when she returned from her walk, he had died. "Everything he loved in one day," she commented sadly.

Our business leaders are just humans with unlimited expense accounts!

* * *

Freehold was sold profitably in the 1980 recession in common with many ICI assets, but my extensive experience with one of the world's largest pension funds got me invited to assist in starting a fledgling company in Canada seeking pension fund investment in real estate.

By the turn of the century, I had become chair of Bentall Kennedy, then one of the most significant investors in real estate for pension funds throughout North America, an association that I enjoyed for many years.

ICI itself had started making losses from 1980 when the world learned to make their industrial products at much lower prices. Many similar large companies were broken up by government action, but ICI did it all to themselves progressively, as their Empire-controlled territories and markets disintegrated.

They were essentially purchased outright by AkzoNobel of Holland in 2007, a highly significant nail in the Empire's coffin!

As a tribute to Norman Freeman's astute investments, the large, independent ICI Pension Fund still operates very successfully from Surrey, United Kingdom, providing benefits to past employees. Billions of dollars' worth of real estate is now owned by the major pension funds throughout the world without question as a matter of good investment policy.

* * *

That first decade in the century which had opened disastrously, with 9/11, the Concorde crash and the stock market collapse, tried to settle down to absorb the new hi-tech civilisation we were developing.

The Blackberry company out of Waterloo, Ontario had created a communication system and produced a few startling technical devices, so when their smartphone came out in 2002, I put in an order. It offered cellular phone service, email capability and internet access, all a total novelty at the time. It was expensive!

Two new obscure online ideas turned up, YouTube and Twitter. Would they succeed?

More strife was on the way!

The Brits had joined America in striking the Taliban in Afghanistan and in 2003 *Tony Blair*, the British Prime Minister, supported America's Iraq invasion. He did this on the mistaken belief they were developing weapons of mass destruction, although they undoubtedly had supported al-Qaeda.

This resulted in a terrorist attack on the London underground at rush hour by four suicide bombers.

Regular life was continuing, however. In 2005 an obscure pretty 14-year-old country folk singer was signed up by Big Machine records. Her name unconventionally, was simply *Taylor Swift,* contrasted to the big stars: *Lady Gaga, Machine, Arctic Monkeys, Black Eyed Peas, Snoop Dog, Beyoncé, Rhianna* and others.

In any event, the prevailing sound was discordant hip-hop, alternative rock and post-grunge.

Dramatist Lane Middleton

When my wife *Lane Middleton* and I met at this time, she was in her forties. I was, well, considerably older; and that was over twenty years ago.

Having totally given up on personal relationships, I unexpectedly had met the love of my life. My stunned, spontaneous first words to her, on a fortuitous blind date, amazingly romantic for an Englishman, were, "My, aren't you lovely!"

Lane was on a long international jaunt, following her lifetime passion for acting, capitalising on her outgoing, vivacious nature and dazzling smile. I quickly learned of her interests in skydiving, horseback riding, skiing, but especially scuba diving and of all things, trapeze.

She graduated from McGill University and worked a happy business career for some twenty years, mainly in public relations, at Seagrams in Montreal, until they moved to New York. She then took an early retirement and set off around the world, acting and seeking adventure.

Over those years in Montreal, she performed in repertory but now she had acting generally in London, then in Los Angeles and now Vancouver.

Then she was lucky enough to meet me, I often joke … carefully!

Although we both enjoy energetic sports and work-out regularly, I quickly found that there was no way I could keep up with Lane.She is inclined to extreme sports which have included for example skydiving, scuba in caves and swimming with sharks, which I avoid.

I found, however, that her exercise program included trapeze training and that at every opportunity we would seek out rigs in various parts of the world for her to perform her various 'catch and releases'.

She particularly enjoys the active Santa Monica pier, but her sport has taken us to seek out rigs at the top of a high-rise in New York, a windy cliff-top Maui and a Canadian mountainside.

Lane was chatting in Vancouver with *Jimmy Pattison*, our local Canadian billionaire who happens to own *The Guinness Book of Records* and he mentioned *Betty Goedhart,* whom they recorded as the oldest living trapeze artist in the world.

On a recent trip to the Santa Monica Trapeze, we went on to La Jolla and Lane visited the fit and energetic 91-year-old, Betty. She started trapeze training in California at 78.

She had always been very athletic! As a youngster she became a featured skater on the London-based Holiday on Ice show and she performed around the world for forty years, after she and her husband had bought out the company.

I am content to stand, in safety, well away from the rig and act as photographer.

* * *

Just to explain myself, the new century had opened miserably for me personally. After my original Bahamian marriage in 1963 we raised our family in Vancouver. Bob is now a prominent King's Counsellor celebrity lawyer, politician and musician. Paul, is a very independent singer, builder and contractor. Sara, a bright academic businesswoman. Guy, who struggled all his life with excessive compulsive mental problems, fell to the demon fentanyl.

Their mother sensibly left me when they had moved on in life, for her first love, a mutual friend from Hong Kong, and my rugger club's scrumhalf. The action continues with my ten grandchildren all successful in their chosen North American ways of life and with Lane's extensive Montreal, London, Los Angeles and Singapore-based family.

With an appalling lack of caution, I had jumped into a second emotional draining and very expensive marriage, fortunately a short experience.

I have never seen the sense of 'retiring'. Retiring is being free to do what you want to do. And I found there were enough celebrities fighting their ways into my life.

Lane and I were setting out on the best years of our lives, which for us has involved remaining fully engaged in business, vocational and charitable activities but increasingly fitting in extensive travel. All of which we tackle with enthusiasm!

Sir Obi-Wan Alec Guinness

I needed desperately to impress Lane with my theatrical interest, but the best I could come up with was my directorship at the local Arts Club Theatre and the time when *Sir Alec Guinness* almost became my brother.

* * *

In a little lane by Winchester High Street in England, just behind the 15th century Buttercross, there was a beautiful little wine bar. There, my widowed father Bob met regularly with his friend *Mrs Agnes Guinness*, for a lunch time snack or after-work tipple.

I met her a few times in the early 1960s on leave from Hong Kong and pulled my father's leg to get on with the relationship because I wanted to be the brother of her son, *Sir Alec Guinness.* She looked older than my father, so it was not likely to happen, but they had become close friends.

My father first met Alec at the wine house in the late 1950s when he was down from London, dressed in a kilt under a raincoat. He normally had a very superior English accent, and my dear old Dad did not have a clue who he was. He had never seen his movies. We learned later that he was filming *Tunes of Glory*, in which he played a Scottish military officer and he liked to live the part.

I always hoped Alec would turn up when I was in Winchester, but he never did, and I had to suffice with Mrs Guinness' tales. She was a good storyteller, had people enthralled around the bar and refilling her glass. Mrs Guinness obviously liked attention and flirted with the men and I worried that getting her serious with my father was a big stretch.

She revelled in everyone calling her Mrs Guinness respectfully, although that was apparently not her formal name. In his autobiography Sir Alec is quite open about his lack of a registered father. His mother, apparently quite a party girl in her youth, was rather too available to the Isle of Wight Royal yachting crowd, became pregnant and produced him in 1914.

No father confessed to the deed on his birth certificate. His mother gave her single name as Agnus Cuff and registered him as Alec Guinness de Cuff. 'Guinness' seems to be a mystery, but a Scottish banker stepped up and paid for his keep and education. It was common in those days for members of the Royal Family and wealthy people to use a surrogate to support illegitimate children. Alec suggests that may have happened; hinting strongly, of course, at Royalty.

* * *

Back in November 1963, I was on a trip to New York, having dinner of course at Sardis and there was Sir Alec dining alone at the next table. He was very much the prominent knighted actor but who had not yet dreamed of Obi-Wan Kenobi in *Star Wars*, which rather strange character earned him an Oscar nomination and made him far more money than the rest of his illustrious career combined.

At the time he was in rehearsal for *Dylan*, which was opening in January 1964 on Broadway. The *maitre d'* of course was all over him and Sir Alec chatted politely with his beautifully calm, modulated voice about theater, his new play and general theatre chitchat.

Naturally, with lowered voice I launched off to my companions on my silly story about almost being Alec's brother and they urged me to go and talk to him. I almost did; half rising at one point.

But Sir Alec was by then immersed in a book, obviously preferring to be on his own. And I decided not to interrupt him. I have kicked myself ever since!

How would the theatrical "Excuse me, Sir Alec. You could have been my brother" work as an opening line? No? Well, maybe just as well, then!

A good story and Lane seemed suitably impressed.

Alec had also made it into the new century but only just. He died August 2000 having performed his last London stage play at the Comedy Theatre in 1989, *A Walk in the Woods*.

However, he had negotiated a 2.25 per cent interest in the revenue of the Star Wars movies! And although he hated the simplistic acting, it grossed billions making Alec internationally famous and of course incredibly wealthy.

Obi Wan Kenobi was still changing the universe in the latest *Star Wars* editions although Alec had been reduced to a somewhat ghostly form!

* * *

Heading to the end of the first ten years, none of that Western World culture was to be seen in Communist China which went overboard in presenting Chinese history and culture at the 2008 Beijing Olympic Games, with all industry closed to reduce the smog, temporarily.

Barack Obama was sworn in as the first Black US President but just in time to take on another major American, and world, financial collapse.

That international financial crash of 2007-08 was led by the Lehman Brothers bankruptcy, again starting in New York.

Fortunately, due to the conservative influence of people like Norman Freeman, the businesses with whom I was associated were well financed and prospered. But all in all, it was quite an interesting opening decade for the new century!

Dexter Morgan

The notorious mass murderer *Dexter Morgan* sighed and looked at me sympathetically. My self-confident and vivacious Lane was uncharacteristically tongue-tied and unable to carry on a cohesive conversation with him. Fictional as he was. She had met many celebrities in business and during her acting career, yet Dexter mesmerised her!

Michael C. Hall had just performed in the New York production *The Realistic Jones*, which concerned mental illness and he possibly thought her afflicted. In fact, she was uncharacteristically dumbstruck.

After graduating from McGill, Lane spent decades in business but continued with her first love, acting, in Montreal repertory theatre, notably appearing in productions by *Steve Galluccio*, later famous for *Mambo Italiano*.

To me a movie or television show is just fiction, but Lane becomes totally absorbed. This happened the moment she met Dexter, and she perceived him as the actual 'justified' murdering television character, Dexter Morgan, he portrayed in the smash hit series by that name.

To her she was actually talking to the character she admired. Something came over her. "This is Dexter," she thought, "my hero." But the words would not come.

He just kindly put a comforting arm around her and took their treasured selfie.

Back in New York the next year, we once again had the opportunity to chat with Dexter, but now as the charming *Michael C. Hall.* When she perceived him as the accomplished actor he is, she was her usual charming articulate self. And Michael felt it was safe to turn his attention towards me, for a moment!

Lane's influence extended to train me to remember actor's names and subsequently, due to her, we rubbed shoulders with several acting notables.

We were sitting in the Air Canada lounge at Los Angeles Airport when a frail gentleman came and sat next to us. Lane immediately engaged super movie star *Martin Landau* in animated conversation, which they were still at in Vancouver, when we helped him pick up his luggage and find his contact. He was very attentive and kindly, but far from robust and surprisingly travelling alone.

He died a few years later in 2017 and we have always regretted we did not arrange to entertain him when he was on that visit late in life.

* * *

We were strolling in Leicester Square, London, when Lane suddenly called, "Chris" and ran across to have an animated conversation with a tall, good-looking fellow. After her chat she just returned smiling happily and said, "That was Chris." I later learned to be *Chris Noth,* Mr Big in *The Sex in the City* TV series.

* * *

Another star who came across us in New York was *David Constable,* who at the time was starring in the TV series *Billions*. We had attended a show in which he performed, and he turned up in the theatre bar for a drink later. Lane was immediately deep in conversation, but being gay, he tactfully gravitated to more convivial company.

* * *

Vancouver being a movie town, acting celebrities turn up all the time. I sat next to *Tom Selleck* at lunch once. *Henry Winkler*, *The* Fonz, (but now he explained, a producer), just casually joining us for a drink one night. And so it goes.

After all, Lane happened to mention nonchalantly she had lunch with *Michael Murphy*, and had associated with *Jane Fonda, David Hemmings, Donald Sutherland, James Spader* and long ago also the same *Henry Winkler*, among others.

Architect Arthur Erickson

I was delighted to have the opportunity to introduce Lane to my longtime friend *Arthur Erickson* fairly early in that new decade. He was well into his eighties and getting a little frail.

He is notably Canada's most famous architect and was still designing, although he did not appear in public very often.

We joined him at a False Creek summer cocktail party, and he was his usual absolutely debonaire, quietly spoken, modestly opinionated self. Lane was of course immediately charmed.

Arthur had met me as far back as 1968 when he was already famous for designing and constructing the Simon Fraser University. I was on the board of Grosvenor Laing, which was building the McMillan Bloedel building in downtown Vancouver designed by his Ericsson Massey architectural firm. So, I got to know Arthur and his business partner Geoffrey Massey well then. It is now the Arthur Erikson Building.

When Stanley Kwok and I started our partnership a few years

later, we were approached by Arthur with a fascinating proposition. The *Dean of Christchurch Cathedral* had asked them to design an internationally outstanding edifice to replace the existing dowdy, impractical 'cathedral' building in the centre of downtown Vancouver.

Arthur asked us if we would act as developers and we set about arranging construction quotes and financing to confirm its financial viability, based upon his design of a startling, high-rise office building with a beautiful modern cathedral individually constructed and identified in the lower floors.

It was the brainchild of the *Bishop* and the *Dean* who worked with us daily on the project, intending to provide the Church with a practical, working city centre facility and income from the office building to finance its activities indefinitely. In 1971 the proposition was put to the church membership which voted enthusiastically in favour of the project.

We set about finishing the design and arranging the construction of the facility which was set to become an international religious icon! After all, Arthur and Geoff became renowned for the Simon Fraser University, the Canadian Embassy in Washington, the Ray Thompson Hall in Toronto, the Museum of Anthropology at UBC and the San Diego Convention Center, among many more architectural triumphs.

However, the 'general public' stuck in their collective long noses, claiming that the old building with its fake buttresses, was of extreme architectural significance to the city.

After years of lobbying, they convinced the City Council to designate 'The Cathedral' as a Class A Heritage Building.

* * *

During the financial damage control, we advised the Dean to sell their development rights to the building next door.

Our friend *Jack Poole OC*, the prominent head of Daon Development (and later famously responsible for bringing the 2010 Winter Olympics to British Columbia) could not believe his good luck. His resulting Park Place next door to the Cathedral has been an extreme financial success, which investment could have benefitted the community.

The disappointed Dean left Vancouver for California having found a more progressive *Jesus* to follow. The Bishop accepted it philosophically as the will of His Father, *God*.

* * *

Naturally I had seen Arthur a lot and we continued to meet on various projects over the years, but I could really only claim him as a good acquaintance rather than friend. He kept his personal life very close to himself. In fact, I never knew his lifetime companion *Francesco Kripacz* and I was much more friendly personally with his practical business partner *Geoff Massey*.

Himself from a celebrity family and with a famous partner, every bit the practical Geoff fully earned all his share of the credits that came to the Erickson Massey partnership.

He grew up in the wealthy and well-known Canadian Massey family, enjoying their fortune made from the massive Massey Ferguson agricultural machinery company. What a business to have in farming giant Canada!

The Massey name graces several prominent buildings, particularly Massey Hall in Toronto.

Geoff's uncle *Vincent Massey* served as a prominent Canadian diplomat and as Governor-General of the country. His father was even more universally well known, *Raymond Massey* the actor.

But Geoff Massey, who lived locally to be 94, had all the attractive physical attributes of the Masseys, tall, handsome and engaging, but he was always just Geoff.

I had assumed that Arthur was gay although the social attitude was different then and I really cannot remember the subject ever coming up. It was obviously never an issue.

Arthur was excited about his cathedral project design and understandably depressed when the project was rejected.

The city missed out on a staggeringly beautiful internationally renowned practical edifice and retained the dowdy, dark little building which the congregation still fantasises as 'The Cathedral'!

Independence

The Empire was beginning to fade into our memory, but connections with friends and stories of the past kept drawing us back. The universal use of English had a lot to do with it, of course, but also an interest and concern at their progress since independence. We were taking an introspective view of the lost Empire.

Senate President Lynn Holowesko

Our first overseas trip together was back to the now very independent Bahamas.

The islands were proving to be one of the more successful of the Empire's lost possessions, benefitting from their proximity to the United States and establishment as a prominent offshore tax haven.

Relaxed Bahamian lawyer, *Jerome Pyfrom*, his sister *Senator Lynn Holoesko* and all their family have been longtime close family friends. We have been back to the Bahamas many times and meet up with Jerry on trips around the world. The Pyfroms were one of the original colonial settlers.

Lane and I were staying in Harbour Island, one of the world's finest small island resorts. We were invited to nearby Eleuthera Island for Jerry and his son Elliot to show us their origins.

We drove by jeep from their old traditional family home on Pyfrom Road (of course) in Governor's Harbour for miles, over land still owned by his family trust, previously planted as pineapple estates until Dole in Hawaii out-planted them.

Finally, we arrive at a rocky area, far from anywhere. He waved us to a hole in the ground, switched on his flashlight and, careful not to spill his gin and tonic, clambering downwards.

There on the wall, in the depths of the cave are the charcoaled names daubed by his forebears, shipwrecked on the island in their move from Germany to the Bahamas in the 1700s. They lost everything, were stranded on an unknown and sparsely populated island and with only that cave in which to shelter.

* * *

Since then, they have prospered somewhat! At Jerry's contractor brother's home way Out East in Nassau I committed the ultimate gauche *faux pas*.

We were being entertained at a pool party which featured free-flowing wine and prize Dobermans leaping into the pool. In the sitting room, in an inconspicuous setting, hung a very striking painting. "That really looks just like a *Modigliani*!" I said cleverly.

"That's because it is a Modigliani," laughed our Pyfrom host.

* * *

Jerome's sister the *Hon. Lynn Holowesko* and late lawyer husband Bill invited us to a dinner party at their beautiful home in gated Lyford Cay at the west end of New Providence Island in 2003.

Lynn is also a top lawyer, a politician and was then serving her six-year term as President of the Bahamas Senate. Early in the century, she had been appointed deputy leader of the United Nations Environmental Law panel and was the longest-serving chair of the Bahamas National Trust. Lynn is brilliant and had always been a beautiful person in all senses since we were young.

We sat regally at her long dining room table being pampered by hovering staff in white gloves. She mentioned, in passing, that it was a pity next-door neighbours *Sean* and *Micheline Connery* had not been available to join us that evening, much to actor Lane's chagrin.

On Lyford Cay residents tend to make nonchalant comments like that about their famous neighbours.

The Pyfroms have come a long way from that hole in the ground!

Big game guide Baby Ice

Now well into my seventies, our life had settled down to at least three months of varied travel during Vancouver's winter months, arranged around my business and social meetings and Lane's acting gigs.

Lane loves cats, so one of our early escapades had to be an African safari. It was not my first.

Back in 1961 Tanganyika was still a colony: just!

It was late in the afternoon when the light plane dropped me in a jungle clearing deep in central Africa with NJOMBE painted on the runway.

Assured someone was coming to pick up the mail, I sat on my suitcase in the airstrip shack listening to strange bird sounds and disconcerting animal noises outside.

Eventually, to my relief, a chatty young Ismaili fellow turned up in a truck and drove me into the small town, Njombe, where I met his father, the only grocery provisions and store owner. Everyone called him Mr Jiwa, respectfully. He knew my planter sister and brother-in-law well. "Peter and Eileen," he nodded. "My boy will happily drive you out to their place."

I was to meet the hospitable Jiwas several times during my visit.

Fifty years later in Vancouver a close friend of ours, herself originally from Tanganyika and a member of the Ismaili community, who had heard my story, said she had someone we must meet. A handsome, now greying, Vancouver lawyer came up grinning, shook my hand and said dramatically, Jiwa!

It was my cheerful truck-driving, fellow Child of the Empire from the jungle.

* * *

My own first close encounter with animals in the wild was on that trip. A local kid on a bike would ride up to tell us where the lions were, and we would rush off in a plantation truck to seek them out and snap some photographs on our Brownie cameras.

As hated white colonialists, Eileen and Peter were ejected from their groomed plantation with no compensation and thrown out of the country, as were the Jiwas, in the later 1960s when the re-named Tanzania had fully gained its independence from the Empire.

* * *

In more recent years, we toured South Africa in style, visiting Soweto and the apartheid museums in the major cities before heading off to Botswana on our main quest: big cats.

My search for lions was to be more sophisticated, and we were advised to pre-reserve a renowned wildlife guide, whom all referred to as Baby Ice, in the Okavango Delta. This ex-Empire territory had been the British protectorate of Bechuanaland but obtained independence in 1966. It is a poor country, but its deltas contain an incredible variety of so far, undisturbed wildlife.*Baby Ice,* and we never heard him referred to differently, met us at the Stanley Camp and we set out driving around alone with him in his small but powerful open truck seeking out every animal going. It was several days before he found us a large pride of lion with youngsters running around. They were resting in the shade under some trees in the bush and we were able to sit quietly and watch their antics for a couple of hours.

Then as the sun went down, we left the lions to find a large clearing for Baby Ice to serve the sundowner. Every afternoon he put up a folding table, covered it with a white cloth, produced Lane's choice – a bucket of champagne and snacks – for the sundown ceremony. We kept a wary eye on the surrounding jungle, ready to jump into the truck if danger presented.

* * *

One morning we were watching hundreds of hippos cavorting in the river, when his radio informed us a white rhino and calf had been sighted, an hour's drive away across very rough country. We hung on for the crazy ride and he found the extremely rare rhinos for the most remarkable sighting of the trip.

We flew from camp to camp, ending up in Zambia, but Baby Ice was the king, although he never found Lane her key objective, a leopard. We spent hours seeking, only to be met by the inquisitive gentle eyes of giraffes watching over the trees.

* * *

The adjacent Zambia had become independent in 1964, and we were in the town of Livingstone to gawk at the Victoria Falls, and compare them to our prized Niagara Falls.

Viewing the statue of the great African explorer David Livingstone in the main square, we asked our local young guide friend why they kept the name and particularly the statue of a colonial oppressor?

He laughed.

"You British think you invented slavery, but it has been going on here forever. Over countless centuries our people were oppressed and taken into slavery by the Arabs from the north. Livingstone actually freed us.

"Some misguided folk tried to have the statue taken down, but they were easily defeated. Tourism and income is more important than worrying about that old colonial stuff," he said with a grin.

And then philosophically, way ahead of his years he added, "We already had slavery before you came and you British were the ones who finally stopped it, weren't you?"

Entertainer Lenny Kravitz

Back in Europe, another Bahamian popped into our lives.

Rome is not always sunny. Lane and I were caught in a heavy rainstorm there in September 2011.We took refuge in the nearest building and seeing a restaurant in the penthouse, up we went. It was actually very smart with white tablecloths and sparkling crystal, so we had a lucky break.

It continued to pelt with rain, and having cracked a bottle of wine we wandered out onto the patio to watch the city, beautiful in the sun and heavy downpour.

We were joined there by a group of animated young people who were shouting happily in English and were having a great time. Back inside, we found them partying at the next table. The rain went on and on with the restaurateur coming around apologetically pouring complimentary drinks, so it was indeed party time!

By then we were chatting happily with them and particularly a young black fellow with neatly trimmed hair, dark shades, wearing an informal, smart jacket. We tried to guess where he was from by his accent, and he said the Bahamas Out Islands.

We asked, "Which one?"

And he answered, "Eleuthera."

"Know it well," we said.

He said, "I still have a house there across from Harbour Island. Look me up next time you are there."

Then he chatted on, "Do you eat at Rock House?" which is the only gourmet restaurant on the island. "One of the happy gay guys that own it died suddenly," he informed us sadly, chatting on about local gossip.

The rain slowed down and one of his companions said, "We really have to get going."

So, he jumped up and said, "Goodbye. Great to meet you. Seriously, please do come and knock on the door in Eleuthera."

He turned to go, and I called after him, "Wait, what's your name?" He replied, "*Lenny Kravitz!*"

Lane exclaimed, "We went to your concert in Hyde Park in London just last week."

"Poor you," he replied, "that was a real washout, wasn't it?" It had also rained heavily during his whole outdoor performance.

Then he was gone, still in the rain.

* * *

Revelling in Empire-style pageantry, London hosted the Olympic Games in 2012 and later celebrated the birth of a second royal baby for the Duke and Duchess of Cambridge, more commonly known in the tabloids as William and Kate. It was a sister for Prince George, as a reserve to ensure the fading Empire's succession traditions.

Bajan Ram Edgehill

My introduction to the Caribbean had been through the Bahamas, but Grosvenor had sent me to the British Virgin Islands to check on their estate holdings there. In many of the colonies, ownership by the past King's pals was evident and the Grosvenors were next to royalty.

These beautiful tropical islands with mainly dirt roads, linked by small bridges were charming and my stay in Tortola was way outside my mundane business life in North America. Naturally, my work there took longer than expected.The islands' rather strange name was selected in a more religious era by Christopher Columbus himself, no less, in honour of Saint Ursula and her 11,000 saintly martyred virgins who would not submit sexually and presumably religiously, to the rapacious Hun.

The archipelago is made up of some sixty islands and small cays, so the name demonstrates Christopher's sense of humour, as much as his religiosity.

They were also wonderful waters for buccaneers, and it was a pirate domain until a group of tough British planters took it over in the mid-1600s. When I visited for Grosvenor, just over three hundred years later different buccaneers were back: bankers. They were moving the Virgins into the clandestine offshore financing business which is now their major industry.In competition, Barbados also advertises that it offers very efficient offshore financial services, completely confidential business incorporation and insurance.

Much as Lane and I enjoy the Bahamas and the Virgins, we have moved on to storm-free Barbados, which had long been a scuba-diving destination for winter-suffering Montrealer, Lane.

It was inevitable, considering their active reefs and Lane's passion for sea creatures. The celebrity dive master, our friend *Ram Edgehill*, takes us out on his ageing boat, *Scotch 'n' Soda*. He is an original, as is his boat!

Lane gets Ram's personal attention on dives, but I worried once when they went off on a nighttime wrecking dive.

They kitted up on a beach in the dark and disappeared off into the sea to explore the wreck. Finally, their glimmering lights reappeared way out in the bay and eventually they returned to drinks and a relieved reception on the moonlit beach.

Of course, diving with Ram in Barbados was generally pretty straightforward and safe but then the risk began. Ram is a party guy, so it was always back to the afternoon beach bar, with bottles of rum, or rum punch for the weak, arriving before the hamburgers.

We would make it back to our apartment, to be awakened late in the evening by thunderous knocking reminding us Ram had reserved us a table at his nightclub. There we danced to his renowned Redman Band with endless margaritas magically appearing. But that is the life in the islands and which they all somehow survive.

Ram claims his forebears in Barbados were the first slaves, which is curious because he appears to be white. The darker members of his band joke that, anyway, if so, he equally comes from white trash.

Barbados was a proprietary colony and originally did not have Crown Land, all ownership just being sold off to the King's pals at the time. The workers went with the land.

If you were a dirt-poor white person from Europe, pressed by poverty to work on the island, as an 'indentured worker' like Ram's ancestors, you were in the hands of the owners. They were joined later, of course, by even cheaper black slaves from Africa, but were soon all in the same fix.

When an 'enlightened' society freed the slaves, they were all out of work with no employment options and nowhere to live. A few sailed off to other islands. The others, like Ram's ancestors, just stayed around and endured the oppression and poverty.

That was long ago and other people. Now they are all equal citizens doing well in life and having a hell of a good time! Some, like Ram, a true Child of the Empire, are even celebrities.

* * *

A short trip to the west we enjoy the tropical islands of St Lucia, St Vincent and Grenada, all of which had to wait a few more years to achieve their independence from the Empire, but are now established high-end tourist areas. Behind the bright sunlight, gorgeous beaches and rolling sea, St Lucia and St Vincent also caught on quickly to offshore banking, while Grenada ran into financial and legal problems and claims to have withdrawn from that dubious business. We will see!

* * *

On the far south side of the Caribbean Sea, there is a curious footnote, with the failed 1698 Scottish attempt at establishing a colony, on what is now the Panama Isthmus.

Scotland itself was still independent at the time but the tragic failure of their Darien Scheme colony, New Edinburgh, with the death by disease of most of their colonists, contributed financially to their forced union with the England in 1707, forming the United Kingdom.

A pity, the country is rugged and isolated, and the Scots could have settled in well. All colonialists do not necessarily win.

Just before being hit by Covid, we went through the Panama Canal and it would have been fun dropping off for a large, iced scotch whiskey on the beach at the nearby Scottish tartan colony, had it succeeded.

Instead, we enjoyed margaritas in still Dutch Aruba, which was also, like so many territories around the world, once British, if briefly, during the Napoleonic Wars.

British influence is evident throughout the entire Caribbean. Aruba, populous Jamaica, and oil rich, but now dangerous to visit, Trinidad, have developed their own distinct characters, but many charming islands such as Barbados, still display the delightful calm of their earlier, relaxed tropical lives.

That laidback lifestyle and history is personified by unique, genuine characters such as generational island celebrity, Ram Edgehill.

Mahatma Anil Hatkar

We had settled down into our 'independence' rhythm, selecting international business, which tied into our interests, taking us away for those several months of Vancouver rain each year.

Our trips were not all just for tourism and in 2014, I was pursuing some business interests in our long-lost Empire territory, India. I had visited that continent on several occasions since 1958 when I sailed grandly into Bombay as a brash young colonial.

This time we were royally entertained. Our celebrity host's sleek, long limousine barely paused as it slid silently through the noisy, dirty road. Street people crowded the sidewalks and slept around the guarded entrance of the exclusive Mumbai Jockey Club.

Inside, we skirted the racetrack and headed for the magnificent clubhouse.

Our gracious host, the eminent architect *Mahatma Anil Hatkar,* personally held the door for Lane and ushered us in for pre-lunch cocktails with his gregarious, happy wife, who wore a beautiful silk sari.

After a sumptuous meal, served by turbaned, silent and attentive uniformed retainers, we toured the club grounds and watched his racehorses training. It all took me back to my colonial grandeur!

Later, we were taken in the limo from the calm, manicured club grounds back into the frantic cacophony that is Mumbai.

Lane and I were disturbed by the hordes of ragged street people and asked the Hatkars whether that bothered them.

"We just don't see them!" he shrugged philosophically.

* * *

Once in India, although 'on business', of course, with Lane's love of cats, it was inevitable that we went on safari again, but this time looking for tigers.

Further north, the famous Ranthambore Reserve is below New Delhi and renowned for its protected tigers, which are rarely sighted.

We were prepared to be disappointed and we sat immobile in the small open truck for hours alone with our guide just listening for the tell-tale sounds and bird calls sounding alarm at the arrival of big cats. But on the first day out we briefly encountered a male and female. The next day our guide found us a celebrity tiger, the notorious *'Number 20'*. This magnificent large male was renowned for having killed three villagers, acceptable under Indian law because they had illegally encroached upon his territory.

'20' stopped and looked us over from 10 feet, shrugged and strolled off leisurely into the bush peeing occasionally to mark his territory.

* * *

On the fifth day we shared a jeep with a couple of visiting senior government officials and with their special authority, went way further into the reserve passing through locked gates into forbidden territory.

The guides located a female and two grown cubs who just majestically strolled up to inspect us and then walked on along the river. We followed and took pictures of them from a reasonable distance for the rest of the afternoon.

The guide went home well rewarded.

* * *

In 1961 *Prince Philip* had been there, safe in a hunting blind. He eased back on the trigger and shot a magnificent strolling tiger. It was in its prime of life and offering no threat to anyone.

Queen Elizabeth applauded fondly at her husband's side and arranged for his trophy to be preserved and displayed back in their country cottage, Windsor Castle, for all to applaud her husband's prowess.

They were entertained at their local palace by the Maharaja and Maharani of Jaipur, who had invited them especially for the kill. Such were the customs of the Empire.

After our passive tiger expedition, Lane and I stayed at the now-converted Rambagh Palace Hotel in Jaipur, revelling in its grandeur and spacious grounds. But being in those surroundings reminded her too much of what she considered the Philip's despicable action.

In the reserve, the tigers were well fed and raised to be totally self-secure, walking right up to our truck, and just looking at us curiously from ten feet or so without any concern. We ourselves may have had a tinge of concern but they were clearly not hungry.

They are completely defenceless to firearms, and there was no excuse for Prince Philip's action or Her Majesty's beaming applause. I consoled Lane that all we could do was write it off to the times and arrogance of the Empire.

She perhaps demonstrated her trust in the species, or more likely was performing as usual, when an enormous female tiger in Thailand later allowed a beaming Lane to be photographed with her arm draped casually over her back. I sensibly cowered on the other side of a viewing window.

* * *

Lane suggested since we were already in the west of India why not just pop over into the Indian Ocean to look at another of our lost Empire territories: The Maldives. She was concerned, with good reason, that their reefs were stressed and the low islands themselves threatened by climate change.

As long ago, as the fifth century BCE – 'Before the Common Era' as the previous 'Before Christ' is now called all-inclusively – records show the Maldives have been colonised by successive maritime powers. Somehow, they managed to retain their more recent Islamic roots but remained plagued by corruption and internal political fighting until the present day.

The British Empire claimed The Maldives in early days and kept them until 1965, although the British military stayed on uninvited as usual.

They had joined the Commonwealth but just before we visited there was considerable political instability reported and the obvious thing was to fly straight from the airport to our resort, Maafushivaru. Just as well because internal squabbles led to their angry withdrawal from the Commonwealth. But they recanted recently, bringing the membership back up to fifty-four nations which demonstrates the original extent of the Empire.

* * *

Being in a Muslim state, we had abided by the highlighted check-in instructions and arriving at Maafushivaru, Lane was dutifully wearing long sleeves and cover-ups. Next morning, to my consternation of course, tiny string bikinis abounded at the beautiful sunlit beach breakfast venue!

Getting into the spirit, Lane and I rented a nearby small island for the day with gorgeous (obviously nudie) soft sandy beaches, set in their turquoise sea. Some accommodating soul had even located an outdoor four-poster bed right on the beach, next to a shack with a stocked bar, snacks and lounging facilities. Very thoughtful.

Lane swam off immediately to snorkel inside the reef, looking for her sea creatures, leaving me sitting safely alone on our long, deserted beach, totally relaxed with a large cool glass of wine in my hand.

Then I saw the big black fin slide up slowly behind her. As she recounts the story it was only a medium-sized reef shark, several of which she had encountered diving previously.

I have reluctantly swum in the water with sharks. Lane coerced me to dive with her outside the reef at Bora-Bora, in Tahiti, unfortunately a French possession, specifically to go down with, I was told, non-aggressive black tipped sharks. But then, we were on honeymoon and I was under severe romantic coercion.

This time, she did not break her stroke and I watched in mounting alarm. She just steadily swam on, secure in her belief that sharks never attack humans in clear water. She came back very excited and unconcerned, if a little tense. It took me a while and the remainder of the bottle before the seductive facilities on the beach started to resume their attraction.

We flew away from the Maldives unscathed, surviving both their sea creatures and their waring politicians. What an absolutely beautiful sadly lost, Empire possession.

Dr W.E.O. Jones, Surgeon

Aussies come from the same social and traditional background, and I have always found them compatible to work with.

While I was with the Land Company in Hong Kong a friendly and gregarious fellow from Australia called *Ron Collier* contacted us.

Like me he was a was a chartered surveyor, but had been sent to Australia by the big London real estate broker Jones, Lang Wootton to set up their office. He was looking for business.

We kept in touch and eventually the Land Company opened an office in Sydney and did a lot of work with him. By then he had opened his own company, of course called Colliers.

Colliers caught up with me again, many years later, when they joined up with Macaulay Nichols Maitland in Vancouver, a venerable Canadian real estate company formed in 1898.

Colliers has expanded internationally and dramatically, now claiming to operate in 66 countries with 18,000 employees working out of 500 offices.

Ron Collier would be amazed at their real estate celebrity status. When he wandered into our Hong Kong office so long ago, he was just a persuasive Aussie realtor, all alone! A Brit seeking his fortune in the Empire.

* * *

One of my own, a working-class grammar schoolboy like me, my pal Willie Jones, also selected Australia, becoming a prominent surgeon there and a celebrity in his own right.

Dr William EO Jones was from Pontypridd in South Wales. His father taught carpentry in the local school.

He excelled at high school, went to Oxford on scholarship, and took his medical degrees at the London Hospital.

We met up at university, became friends and partied together for several years before I headed off to Hong Kong and he to Australia to seek our fortunes.

The English class system has so many affectations. When he finished his medical degree, he proudly called himself Dr Jones, but with weird English perversion, when he became a surgeon, he reverted to Mr Jones. Just another strange English class game. Surgeons have to show they are superior to mere doctors and revert to Mr!

The Aussies are more down to earth, and when he arrived at Port Macquarie on the east side of Australia to invest in a private hospital, he reverted to Dr W. E. O. Jones, although he was at the time the only specialist surgeon in the region.

Later he was acclaimed as 'a giant in the development of medicine in the mid-North Coast' and as 'a brilliant surgeon and wonderful raconteur'.

An invitation from Willie and Margaret started our various vacation trips to sunny Australia, which conveniently provides reverse seasons from Canada. And endless sandy beaches, sea and reefs.

During our college years in London, Willie had introduced me to the game of rugby. Strangely, rugby was a working-class sport in Wales, and he was the star scrum half for London Hospital and Woodford. We continued a close friendship all his life.

* * *

Lane and I could just as easily have settled in Australia rather than Canada. We enjoy the Australian directness and sense of humour. Jokes about convicts have naturally worn a bit thin, although the early development of Australia was unique in the annals of the Empire. And we found it so much easier to colonise large countries with fewer people around to object.

Australia was totally colonial from the original penal colony in 1788 and remained as six distinct colonies until combining itself at the beginning of the last century in 1901 as the Commonwealth of Australia, a self-governing Dominion but still very British.

They were still very much British colonial into the 1970s, particularly with the help of the White Australia Policy, intended to stop them from getting swamped by immigrants from nearby highly populated countries.However, at the end of the last century after a hundred years associated with royalty, they held a referendum to replace the Queen, unbelievably by a lowly president.

The referendum was only narrowly defeated, and King Charles continues tentatively as the head of state.

* * *

Next door, New Zealand, pretty much the same size as its 'mother country' the United Kingdom, also became a Dominion just after Australia, but has never questioned the Crown, at least formally.

One of the most exciting experiences we have had is flying New Zealand's South Island's Southern Alps and its dramatic fjords in a light plane! We hate to admit it, they challenge the Canadian Rockies!

"While we are here," said Lane, "we might as well do some scuba diving in the exquisite Cook Islands." They are still named, of course, after our intrepid Pacific explorer and Empire builder, Captain James Cook! But it seems appropriate that the friendly, laidback islands will one day revert to their own name, Rarotonga.

* * *

Closer to Canada, of course, we have the tropical Hawaiian Islands to visit. With all those beautiful possessions grabbed in Empire days, why had Britain not also snapped up Hawaii, one of west coast Canada's favourite destinations?

The answer is that Britain did once, but after protest from America, backed significantly by a bigger nearby navy, they gave it up again a mere six months later.

Also, the Hawaiians had in early days bumped off the revered Captain Cook on one of his Pacific cruises, so they were definitely troublemakers.

The Empire left them to the Americans, who also eventually themselves in effect colonised them, but providing their enriching tourism bonanza. Otherwise, they might have later provided a welcomed warm province for Canada.

Speaker John Fraser

When I arrived in Canada, I thought I was about done with colonies. I had no idea I would be witnessing the previous colonies of Canada still arguing between themselves in a supposedly self-governing country. The early Canadian colonial territories were, and still are, fighting out their differences.

One constant remained, the Queen.

The Royal Family has maintained a curious relationship with Canada, essentially a fiction. The Speaker of the National Parliament, *Hon. John Fraser*, came to address the Canadian Club in Vancouver when I was Chair.

At lunch, as was our custom, I proposed the Loyal Toast, "Ladies and gentlemen, *Her Majesty the Queen*."

The assembly lumbered, chairs scrapping, to their feet and dutifully repeated the words, sipping their mainly water, lunchtime drink symbolically. So Canadian!

When we were seated for a pause, awaiting his talk, the Speaker leaned across to me and corrected me courteously, "John, the toast should be to Her Majesty, the Queen *of Canada.*"

He was gently pointing out that our beloved *Queen* is somewhat mythical and not the physical person of the *Queen of the United Kingdom*. That leaves the status of the rest of the Royal Family shrouded in mystery.

The Honorable John Fraser, an eminent parliamentarian, served as Speaker of the House of Commons in the landslide Conservative Mulroney government.

A Privy Councillor, and a longtime Member of Parliament, he represented Vancouver South for more than twenty years, during which time he was a Federal Minister and an Ambassador to the United Nations. Notably, he was the highly respected and popular Speaker of the House of Commons until his retirement from Parliament in 1994.

Over all those years John was constantly in the thick of the constitutional debate and an eloquent, if sometimes pleasantly loquacious, speaker on the subject.

Fifteen international territories now call King Charles their head of state, likely because they do not know quite how to change the situation. Australia tried by referendum once, and narrowly failed. Canada would find the need for provincial approval, required public and Indigenous participation and much more, a daunting task.

The situation had been building up for a long time and the problem was all colonial. A couple of years prior to America pulling out, the English Parliament had defensively passed the Quebec Act, already giving concessions and consolidating their position in, what would become, Canada.

Having lost America, they prudently moved to consolidate their four northern colonies. But it was a long time before their North America Act could set up Canada in 1867, including New Brunswick, Nova Scotia, Ontario and French-speaking, Catholic Quebec, always the outlier.

Gradually more colonies joined, Manitoba, far away British Columbia, promised a rail connection, Prince Edward Island, and Northwest Territories then the Arctic Islands. Alberta and Saskatchewan and much later, after the Second World War, Newfoundland.

That Canada was still controlled by Great Britain, was not my Empire's fault. The Balfour Declaration had given all the other dominions their constitutions back, but Canada actually asked to be left out of the Act because they could still not agree internally on new terms.

At least, after the Second World War, the Canadian Supreme Court became the final Court of Appeal ousting the Judicial Committee of England's Privy Council.

Quebec brought matters to a head with their narrowly defeated plebiscite, essentially seeking separation, and the Canadian Government finally petitioned the Queen to patriate the constitution to Canada, allowing full independence from Britain after over a hundred years of internal bickering.

With Pierre Trudeau's persistence a deal was reached, but then rejected by Quebec. The Patriation Agreement went ahead without them anyway, but the Distinct Province, although still being far from happy, negotiated a better deal for themselves.

Finally, the Canada colonies had formed a formally unified country, with its very own constitution and was able to stand on its own feet.

John Fraser, at the time a mere member of Parliament in the Progressive Conservative opposition party, was there April 17, 1982, on Parliament Hill, to witness Queen Elizabeth, patriating the constitution, and signing the Canadian Charter of Rights and Freedoms, before thousands of enthusiastic subjects.

Her Majesty was actually there in person for the ceremony, demonstratively and no doubt with relief, finally freeing her squabbling colonies. And still the Queen of Canada!

Conclusions

The end of the century had seen the handing back of almost all the possessions of the British Empire. Those territories that now remained associated with Great Britain did so for their own good reasons; Anguilla, Bermuda, British Antarctic, British Indian Ocean, British Virgin Islands, Cayman Islands, Falkland Islands, Gibraltar Montserrat, Pitcairn, Henderson, Ducie and Oeno (Pitcairn)Islands.

And the Commonwealth of Nations were doing just fine with their new association!

Old boy Thomas Gainsborough

Britain had notoriously plundered the Empire for valuable historic memorabilia, which stuff their museums. Some treasures from the homeland which had been distributed out previously managed to return! Gainsborough's *Blue Boy* painting was one of these, if only returning for a vacation back home.

The expanding Kilroy real estate business had taken us regularly to California. *Jim Kilroy* was one of the largest developers in Southern California and a renowned maxi-yacht sailor.

Once, he called our board meeting half-way between Hong Kong and Manila, which required me to crew on *Kialoa*, his hundred-foot maxi racing sailboat, one of the world's fastest, on the China Sea race. I was an enthusiastic weekend sailor myself in Vancouver, so it proved the perfect board meeting.

* * *

The late Jim Kilroy would be amazed at the tens of billions of dollars his company now commands.

When his son John Kilroy Jnr eventually took over management of the company at the turn of the century, he invited me as a director, resulting in many years of adventure in California and other parts of the world. This was usually with Lane along and cemented our close relationship friendship with John and Catherine, whose Malibu wedding featured earlier.

Lane knew that the artist *Thomas Gainsborough* was a celebrity Old Boy (among others) who had gone to my school in Sudbury, and on this California visit she went with me to the Huntington Museum in San Marino, where his famous *Blue Boy* painting is on permanent exhibition.

Memories of the bronze-eyed Gainsborough statue still haunt me, but Lane had also been to Sudbury in England and gazed up into his haunting eyes.

We stood an unusually long time in front of the life-sized painting while I knowledgably pointed out details to her (having carefully researched them in advance). We were approached by a uniformed curator who seemed a little concerned at our prolonged interest.

"Did you know there was a dog down there?" I asked him, pointing to the left side of the blue velvet-clad legs, where there was now painted a pile of rocks. He glanced quickly at the vacant space by the boy's feet and started edging protectively in front of his painting. The missing dog is apparently clear on modern X-rays.

"How did you know that?" he asked? I replied, "Because the artist went to my high school. He painted the dog out later." Then I added, I thought humourously, "We had a very good art program."

The guard now looked around for support, but Lane took my arm firmly and moved me to the far end of the gallery, to view Thomas Lawrence's *Pinky*, an equally beautiful painting of a young woman in pink and white.

My Sudbury Grammar School was founded more than 500 years previously by William Wood and the young Thomas Gainsborough did indeed get his education there when his uncle was the headmaster. They surely must have had something of an art programme?

"Trouble-maker!" Lane muttered.

Blue Boy *was happy to return to his home in London in 2022, on loan to the National Gallery.*

But his creator, Thomas Gainsborough, would have been upset to learn that all those fine Grammar Schools, which had so successfully provided the loyal clerks of the Empire, had been closed at the end of the 1980s. They had been converted to more egalitarian, soulless, Comprehensive Schools.

The discipline and character building of the old Grammar Schools were no longer needed.

But Thomas's depleted Sudbury Grammar School Old Boys Association still keeps the cherished memory alive.

Rugby Great, Tokkie Smith

Sevens Rugby is now an exciting Olympic sport played widely by all races around the world.

But in the days of my Empire, it was almost exclusively an establishment, amateur white man's game. *Tokkie Smith* had been raised on South African apartheid and he was intent upon changing all that. It was to cost him everything, including his life.

* * *

Tokkie Smith, yet another child of the Empire, did his own thing and he sure had chutzpah. He would have loved Lane.

At Lantau Airport in Hong Kong, behind thousands, we waited to go through passport control. Lane indicated a kiosk, 'Diplomatic and special passes'.

"Nexus?" she suggested.

I replied in scorn, "That booth's for diplomats. And Nexus only works in North America, anyway."

She replied, "Well let's try."

She marched confidently past the armed guard pointing to her Nexus card and up to the kiosk. I followed assertively. What else could I do?

The bored official looked up from her book, glanced at the waved passes and stamped our passports. We were through!

We use carry-ons and have never checked a bag, even on long trips. So, we jumped into a limo and headed off for the Mandarin Hotel.

* * *

Back again in the Football Club, I realised I had not followed Hong Kong rugby since 1978, when I had last visited my old pal Tokkie.

We had spent almost a decade together in Hong Kong playing for the Club and administering rugby in Asia.

He had subsequently died quite young back in South Africa but certainly had become a celebrity. Now he was a pariah, scarcely remembered. Why?

When we last met, he had just founded and managed the first three extremely important Hong Kong International Sevens tournaments, starting the entire mixed-race international Sevens sport. The press literally called him Mr Rugby.

Why had he been excluded from rugby history? A Sevens official kindly bought lunch, but warned to leave the subject alone. He suggested ominously, "Don't open a can of worms!" Now this really got my attention!

I started corresponding with old rugby acquaintances around the world and slowly the story emerged. But was Tokkie a saint or a sinner?

Granted he drank heavily, he liked the ladies, had affairs and was always on the edge of bankruptcy. But it appeared his rugby activities, especially the Sevens, were highly successful.

Thereafter his status in the game progressively diminished.

Then, Britain still considered itself an imperial power.

Establishment Scotland held a centennial International Rugby Sevens tournament in Edinburgh in 1973. All the players were white!

Considering the brilliant rugby being played by the recently freed Pacific Islanders, did it not occur to anyone to invite a truly representative racial mix? It could have been a symbolic end to blatant colour prejudice of the Empire!

Tokkie and his Hong Kong colleagues then become highly unpopular with the United Kingdom rugby establishment by holding the first ever mixed-race, sponsored, international rugby tournament, particularly showcasing the brilliant Pacific Islanders!

His story was proving so fascinating it led me to write a history, *Tokkie Smith and the Colour of Rugby. Creating the Hong Kong Sevens,* published on Amazon Kindle Books.

His reputation is established in South Africa, where his story has been subject to national television attention, but he still awaits full recognition in Hong Kong.

Wikipedia: "A.D.C. 'Tokkie' Smith was chairman of Hong Kong Rugby Union

1973-1978 and is recognised for his long service to Rugby Asia and for founding and managing the first three Hong Kong International Sevens tournaments."

But I had discovered this was just the beginning of the Tokkie saga. The worst was yet to come.

Tokkie abhorred apartheid, and in 1982 he decided to confront it personally! It was the right ethical decision but catastrophic for him personally.

Arranged in great secrecy, Tokkie's Dragons were the first multi-racial rugby side ever to tour South Africa, playing its powerful provincial sides which finally fielded token black players.

The tour was a big success but on return to Hong Kong, Tokkie and *Chris Wynne-Potts*, a star police and colony player, were excluded from all future rugby. Further, they were, ostracised from society, lost their careers and then forced out of the colony.

Tokkie lost everything, including his business and wife, took to drinking even more heavily, and died young in a car crash.

South African Chris, became a friend, flying to London to meet us, and contributing considerably to Tokkie's re-establishment.

* * *

What happened to Tokkie was symbolic of the Empire: self-interest and money.

Hong Kong, then very much a British possession, subscribed to the Commonwealth Gleneagles Agreement, which decreed that amateur sports teams may not visit apartheid South Africa.

Hong Kong did not at that time yet have Chinese fellows playing the game in the colony. They did not select a Chinese member of the national squad for another 15 years.

Tokkie had picked a terrible place and time to make his personal anti-apartheid statement!

Hong Kong was literally the end of the Empire for Great Britain. Its six million population constituting more than ninety per cent of the remaining subjected people. And Communist China was intent upon taking them.

More than thirty countries had left the British Empire and joined the Commonwealth of Nations. Now the Commonwealth itself was what mattered!

Hong Kong was also in delicate negotiations with Communist

China about the future of the colony. They desperately needed the support of the Commonwealth.

Into that arena stepped Tokkie Smith, defying them all.

Then, to make things worse, Margaret Thatcher went to Beijing in 1982 on her critical visit, the very year poor Tokkie chose to take his forbidden, widely publicised, rugby group to apartheid South Africa in defiance of the Commonwealth!

The politically charged atmosphere doomed Tokkie. This clearly had nothing to do with any racial ethics, but totally to do with politics and money.

The next year Tokkie Smith was ruined and forced out of the colony, and two years later he was dead.

Such was my Empire!

I can see him now, nursing his pint of beer, smiling his engaging smile, and shrugging at all the fuss!

Sportsman Song Koon Poh

Researching the 'Tokkie' book involved more welcomed international travel and meeting friends. A key contributor who initially suffered a similar trial to Tokkie's, and a battle with the Commonwealth, was *Song Koon Poh,* a successful businessman and a well-known traditional Sportsman of the Year in Singapore.

While assembling his Dragons, Tokkie had approached players from Australia, Canada, the United States and the Pacific Islands.

But he had to have a Chinese player.

There were then no Chinese players in white racist Hong Kong rugby and his relationship with their Rugby Union and rugby in Asia precluded him from canvassing their teams. He purposely avoided implicating them because of the Commonwealth Gleneagles edict. Hence, the obviously non-official team name, Tokkie's Dragons!

Then, in the bar, after a Hong Kong Sevens game, he lucked into *Song Koon Poh.*

* * *

We had corresponded with Koon Poh about the Dragons tour and its aftermath while writing *Tokkie*, and he insisted to Lane, we must visit him and he would take us to lunch at his famous Singapore Cricket Club, right in the centre of the city.

What more historical ex-colonial sporting venue anywhere. We sat in awe being entertained and introduced around by one of Singapore's most famous Sportsman of the Year.

This lunch was soon after the rugby book was published, but way back in the 1980s things had been different for Koon Poh, who had found himself a social outcast.

He had been famous as the captain and star player of Singapore's rugby team and had recently captained them in the new Hong Kong Sevens. Contrary to colonial Hong Kong, Singapore had encouraged mixed-race 'character-forming' rugby since English educated Lee Kuan Yew originally took over as Prime Minister.

The rugby tour had been an outstanding success, notwithstanding the privations and annoyances of apartheid. Being obviously Chinese, he was forever searching for a washroom he could use, without upsetting some apartheid sensitivity. Assisted by Poon's strong play, the Dragons won most of their games.

Upon returning to Singapore, Koon Poh learned that he had been ignominiously stripped of his Sportsman of the Year title and banned from any further sporting involvement in Singapore. He was accused of violating Singapore's agreement with the British Commonwealth of Nations not to send sporting teams to South Africa during apartheid.

His employer, Shell Company thought this hypocritical, as Singapore itself was continuing to trade heavily with South Africa and they maintained his career-long senior employment.

It was several years before things quietened down politically, all was forgiven, and Song Koon Poh regained his title and the status in society he so much deserved.

Singapore is one of our most popular destinations and we stay at the famous Tanglin Club which I visited on my first trip to Singapore as a colonial youngster.

Unfortunately, Lane missed out on the famous Long Bar at Raffles Hotel which was closed for renovation. We have a date there with Koon Poh next time to enjoy the Empire's most celebrated drink, The Singapore Sling!

Lt Gov. Judith Guichon

We were surprised when the United Kingdom adopted Brexit in

2016 and when *Donald Trump* was elected the next year to be President of the United States.

Lane and I spent a lot of time in California but since it was one of the strong Democratic states we had become convinced *Hillary Clinton* was going to make it. We had attended some of her rallies and while not totally convinced, absolutely preferred her to Donald Trump.

Our daughter *Sara D'Eathe MBA* had met Donald Trump socially many years previously in New York and had found him charming if totally self-absorbed. At the time she was working in New York following her Master's Degree in business from the Sloan School at MIT.

Sara was employed in New York before the Lehman Brothers and market collapse and returned to Boston to continue her business career. She married Bostonian financier *Rob Leggat*, paused during her family raising years and is now very successfully back in business in Oregon.

Donald Trump was installed as President, but far more significance to us was the election of our son, *Robert D'Eith KC* as a member of the British Columbia Legislative Assembly.

Bob is a prominent entertainment lawyer, recording pianist and author who opted to serve his community in politics. Yes, he had made a further personal change to the name; sensibly to D'Eith removing all oblique reference to death.

Our personal highlight was our visit to Victoria with his wife *Kim* to attend his installation and the opening of the BC Parliament by the *Hon. Judith Guichon* at the grand Parliament Building.

* * *

But by absolute coincidence, to my blushing delight, as the sun was sinking rapidly on our territories, your modest Child of the Empire finally received a personal and appreciated recognition from *Her Majesty, The Queen of Canada.*

I suspect that she may perhaps not quite have known personally, as my Sovereign's Medal for Volunteers, an actual pin-on gong with a distinctive ribbon, in the old military Empire style, was awarded to me by her representative *Hon. David Johnston,* Governor-General of Canada.

Well, even more remotely, it was pinned on me third hand by the gracious *Lt Gov. Judith Guichon* in her Government House. Typical of the province she is a prominent rancher whose family had managed cattle in the Nicola Valley since settlement days. My active service in a surprising two dozen non-profit charitable organisations, during my then fifty-year Canadian career, was kindly recognised. We joined many celebrities from all over British Columbia who had engrossing tales of personal service to the community to tell. And we were indeed treated as celebrities, at least for an afternoon!

* * *

We were soon back in New York to pay our respects, when the new World Trade Centre and sobering museum had opened.

Parts of the world were, however, getting more liberal. For example, the US Supreme Court approving same-sex marriages following Canada and England's example at the turn of the century. And the UK boasted its first female bishop!

The extraordinarily normal, brilliant entertainer, Taylor Swift had taken the lead in the music world, but the young Canadian Justin Bieber was breathing down her neck.

We were relieved when two hundred nations put together the first accord to combat climate change.

But, more important, we now had our very own in-house celebrity, Bob D'Eith KC. MLA!

Bank chair Sir Willie Purvis

Chris Wynne-Potts has flown several times from South Africa, to meet us in London. He had been close to Tokkie through the rugby drama, was a member of the Dragons touring team and at the time lost everything himself on return to Hong Kong.

It helped considerably when he found a stack of old documents in South Africa, 'The Tokkie papers', including some rugby union minutes from that time that held records of the actual firing. Remarkably, the Rugby Union in Hong Kong lost all its formal Colonial historical minutes and records 'in an office move', which would have produced vital evidence of those years.

But the minutes we found, revealed the name of a *W. Purves*, who had spoken at the meeting and voted for the permanent exclusion of Tokkie Smith from further connection with the Rugby Union. He is recorded as recommending, "That the HKRFC dissociate itself from the whole affair including Mr Smith."

He is none other than a young *Sir Willie Purves*, later chairman of the HSBC group, the Hongkong and Shanghai Banking Corporation of my colonial youth, now the major sponsor of Sevens Rugby throughout the world.

We were at a dinner in London before Covid, attended by Sir Willie and his convivial wife Beckie, and chatted with him about the Tokkie affair.

Back at the time of Tokkie's downfall, Willie was already a senior member of the establishment. After a highly decorated military career in Korea, he had arrived in Hong Kong several years before even my appearance there. A top manager, he was eventually chair of the entire bank, retiring at the end of the century.

He knew about the book, which was published the previous year, and we chatted for a while about what he remembered of the event. I arranged to send him a copy.

Sir Willie kindly responded later that he had enjoyed reading the book although he did not concur with the conclusions. He did not elaborate.

The book is written as a history, and expresses the conclusions reached by the press and commentators at the time, but I must admit my sympathies had gone over wholeheartedly to Tokkie, who was adamantly anti-racist and undoubtedly meant well. He was dealing with an all-powerful, hypocritical elite who were protecting their own vested interests, but appear to me, at the time, to have over-reacted.

* * *

We enjoy our regular trips to London where we both have close family but now we also had a rugby book to promote and revived friendships to pursue.

We found the Royal Family remained very much in the news, with Harry bringing a woman of colour into the family, provoking unidentified Royal comment. The undaunted elderly Queen still appeared at Ascot for the races despite the heavy rain.

Little prince Louis was growing into a person and Charles good-naturedly appeared on the *Bond* film set. Then little Archie was born in the States. Dutchess Camilla appeared popularly playing ping-pong at an Air Force party.

My Empire seemed to have slipped from the news!

Casino tycoon Stanley Ho

Again before Covid, risking the political unrest, we went back in Hong Kong. We were getting concerned about visiting on account of the pro-democracy marches and police reaction, which was getting violent.

We were delighted to be invited back for dinner at the venerable Hong Kong Club, which was founded with the colony, and had accepted me as a very junior member in my early days in the colony.

In Hong Kong philistine style, the beautiful original club building had been demolished to be replaced by a standard office tower, but which also contained an opulent new club.

There, in customary surroundings, we were entertained to a long gourmet dinner in the beautiful Red Room overlooking Statue Square and the city lights, by a local businessman who had recently retired from a top position in a large Asian company.

We got onto the subject of kickbacks and bribery of government officials in China and Asia. Our friend laughed that nothing had changed and that it had in fact been his job to dispense such payments.

"Millions?" Lane asked, always curious about inducements.

He laughed ruefully and said, "I wish. Hundreds of millions; every year. There are no major business deals of any type made in the Middle East or the Orient which do not involve serious kickbacks at some level. It is the way of life."

If I had stayed in Hong Kong, it is inevitable I would have done business the same way.

Trying not to sound too goody-goody I assured him I had been involved in many tens of billions of dollars of real estate investment in North America, with no money, I knew about, changing hands illegally or in a dubious way.

Still, we were prepared to accept a few more glasses of excellent Champagne from an apparently unethical source!

* * *

We continued around the world back through London.

I had been growing concerned about the deteriorating business ethics in many of the previously Empire countries, amid increasing alarm about international money crime and laundering affecting

Canada. The discussion in Hong Kong had got me thinking about the situation.

At an event we attended in London a prominent European banker and his wife happened to sit next to us. I knew from press reports that his bank had, a few years before, been dinged $1.9 billion, very publicly, by the American government for money-laundering offences as a middleman for the Mexican drug cartel.

Just that week Deutsche Bank was getting into trouble again for laundering billions of Russian rubles, ING had been fined nearly a billion pounds, Credit Suisse many millions and so on. The indication was that the banks were deeply involved in dubious money flowing around the world. I asked the banker how this happened?

He prevaricated, switched subject couple of times and then eventually said, "No senior banker will discuss whatever that subject is you're trying to raise!" He shook his head decisively. Then he reverted to sport. "Tell me more about your rugby book!" he asked, firmly changing the subject.

Then, during Covid the issue of dirty money came home publicly to Canada and my home province with the Cullen Inquiry into Money Laundering, especially aiming at casinos and my own real estate industry.

* * *

I quickly discovered that the entire subject of money crime in Canada, and its subsequent crime of money-laundering, was totally shrouded in mystery.

We had almost perfect systems for criminals to hide and obscure their identity or investments, and no one had a clue who was actually involve or indeed how much money.

The Provincial Cullen Inquiry, budgeted at twenty million dollars, emerged mainly as an expensive public relations gesture, freely admitting,

"While it is not possible to put a precise figure on the volume of illicit funds laundered through the BC economy each year, available evidence shows that the figure is very large, with estimates in the billions of dollars per year in this province alone."

At least he acknowledged there was a problem. The recognised then current source of dubious money was seen as coming from Communist China, much being via Hong Kong and Macao!

Although it is significant in day-to-day dealing, most money-laundering is not conducted in cash, and obviously our banks and legal systems are heavily involved. They are rarely challenged and never prosecuted. One might ask why?

While it had been suggested I write a factual report on the subject, I could find no hard evidence, which of course is the whole point!

I decided, wisely, to have more fun and express my international experience and feelings in a cynical, historical novel form, which became *Laundering the Dragon. Black Renminbi.*

The original focus of the Cullen Inquiry was the British Columbia gambling industry, which was embarrassingly bringing in billions of tax income for the government, but was highly suspected of illegal financial practices involving money-laundering.

There were rumours and stories and even books written about the Macau casinos' connection, involving outlandish tales of bags of cash and other money forms used by Asian gamblers, emerging as purely laundered Canadian investment funds.

I know nothing about gambling, and I decided to look up my old friend *Stanley Ho* in Macao, who was undoubtedly the world's top gambling authority.

But I was too late!

You did not need fiction or Orson Welles movies to find dubious characters operating in Hong Kong and Macao. Banks are said to be the modern-day pirates.

Way back in my early colonial days in Hong Kong, I was promoted and became seriously involved in developing business contacts of all sorts. Some were of admittedly creative character! One was a new business partner from the unruly gambling Macau. His name was *Stanley Ho.*

I had already become personal friends with a young Macanese fellow called Roger Lobo, and his wife Margaret, later *Sir Roger* and *Lady Margaret Lobo.* Many years later Rogie was to move the 'Lobo Motion' demanding debate in the Legco before Britain and China reached a final deal on the future of Hong Kong.

The Lobos were helpfully close to Stanley, and we were soon out partying together. The wealthy Lobos had notoriously controlled Macau business and gambling for generations, but Rogie now lived a 'normal' Hong Kong life. *Stanley Ho* was destined to take their family place as the tsar of Macau gambling.

Colourful does not even start to describe Stanley Ho's life as the multi-billionaire controller of Macau's extended casinos, and all that entails!

When we first had dinner, Stanley was just building his real estate empire and at the age of 38 was a mere multi-millionaire. Typical of Macau's mixed population going back to the original Portuguese colony in the 1400s, he was of Dutch-Jewish, English and Chinese ancestry and claimed Bosman as a family name, but his Asian eyes and colouring clearly defined his Chinese ancestry.

Stanley started out during the Second World War smuggling goods into China. An Aussie friend of mine flew one of the Lobo family's small planes still smuggling cigarettes and other undisclosed goods around Asia and occasionally into China.

Stanley was a tall, charming, and chatty fellow. At my first social occasion with him he was accompanied by his very young and remarkably beautiful second wife Lucinda Laam. Second 'wife' but Stanley was reportedly still married to Clementine, the mother of his earlier children, but now incapacitated from a car crash. Macau still allowed more than one wife under the Qing Dynasty law. Apparently, Clementine was not amused, but there it was.

That evening he was obviously very close with Lucinda, and they did eventually have five children. They were renowned as a stylish dancing couple and were often in action at our charity events, full of energy.

Much later, he married Lena as his third 'wife', producing three more children and then quickly did it again with Angela his fourth 'wife' with four more kids. He was a man of upstanding energy and many talents, ending up with seventeen offspring!

He declared them all his wives, supported by the ancient Macao Chinese law, which a gambling mogul, multi-billionaire can naturally do. This was eventually much to the delight of his succession lawyers.

Lucinda turned up in Vancouver in 1985 looking after her ageing father and amicably managing Stanley's impressive real estate properties in the city.

Stanley's life was not without its disconcerting, deadly moments in a crime-ridden place like Macau and with the need to please the corrupt Communist dictators in Beijing, especially when you control multiple gambling hotels. They gave him gambling licences and dictatorship of Macau casinos for thirty years. The only gambling licences issued in all China. The mind boggles at the corruption probably involved.

Stanley had his stressful moments, but hey, that goes with being a gambling overlord with him having up to nineteen casinos at last count!

Back then when we were young, Stanley had been just a charming relaxed young guy, enjoying life and having lot of fun. It appears he had never changed.

I thought about looking him up again and maybe visiting? My long-ago acquaintance was undoubtedly the world's top casino tycoon. I could ask him what was going on.

Just a friendly lunch about old times between friends might lead to an illuminating discussion.

But he very ill in hospital in Hong Kong. I was indeed too late!

Stanley had suffered a serious stroke several years before and had languished since then in hospital never recovering. He died soon after, so enormously wealthy no one has been able to calculate his worth, or no doubt locate all his fortune.

Premier David Eby

Hon. David Eby KC became leader of the provincial New Democratic Party and Premier of British Columbia.

While he was still Attorney General in the John Horgan government, he vigorously and passionately attacked the principle of money crime.

He was eloquent and justifiably angry at the previous government's lack of action to address and reduce the risk of criminal activities and subsequent money-laundering, especially evident in British Columbia's gambling facilities.

It was perfectly clear that the federal government was proving itself completely inept or unconcerned at controlling money crime in Canada, as is their duty.

British Columbia's problem was nevertheless just part of a major international criminal phenomenon, which to a certain extent had developed out of the wind-down of the Empire.

It was all to do with criminally inclined offshore banking and investment which was now expanding internationally.

For decades Panama and in Europe, Switzerland, Luxembourg and Cyprus, had been known havens for hidden money, although the European Community was now proving downright uncooperative to these traditional financial scams. Then after the Second World War the number of available countries and states available round the world expanded progressively.

This was demonstrated at this time when the notorious Panama Papers exposed damning information but with little result when a disgruntled law firm employee in Panama decided to publish his company's secret files for the world to read. Millions of records were exposed naming hundreds of politicians, celebrities and businesspeople around the world. Not surprisingly the law firm went out of business promptly and the accounts moved to more prudent operators, but it proved just a slightly annoying glitch and the international offshore industry carried on unhindered. The whistleblower has so far managed to remain anonymous, lucky for him, or her!

While a significant number of Canadian celebrities were named and exposed, no action was taken, and no one was publicly inconvenienced.

Many of the previously Empire, now Commonwealth nations, fitted perfectly into this pattern. It made sense. For the inhabitants of the smaller nations leaving the Empire and searching for income, this had provided a golden opportunity.

Many had operated offshore banking since after the Second World War under cooperative British direction, so they knew the system. Now, they could write their own laws, expand offshore business, and offer confidential services and even protective citizenship to the clandestine wealthy of the world, for a price naturally.

They offered the ability to hold capital in various currencies, to protect investments from home country taxes, associates and spouses, but providing total privacy and security. What more could the oligarchs and capitalists of the world desire?

While the traditional offshore countries remained prominent, the new competition had been provided from the Empire: Antigua, Bahamas, Barbados, Belize, British Virgin Islands, Cayman Islands, Hong Kong, Jamaica, Mauritius, Seychelles, Singapore. Plus self-ruling Bermuda. And the current stars, achieving independence as late as 1983, St Kitts and especially the aggressive tiny Nevis.

Conveniently for them, all the Commonwealth offices are in London, business is conducted in English and the nearby City of London provides experienced, efficient and confidential international financial services to the world.

The flow of dirty money around the world had become a major international industry. Canada and British Columbia were getting their share, now conveniently being hidden within the non-intrusive Canadian financial and registration systems.

The Canadian money-laundering laws, of course, forbade the use of criminally acquired assets, but few business criminals were prosecuted.

At that time, an unhindered flow of capital into Canada, particularly from Communist China, often accompanying immigrants, was distorting the real estate and other markets, causing the Provincial government to become very concerned.

Attorney General David Eby determined to do something about it.

He declared, "We will turn British Columbia and Vancouver into a model for fighting money-laundering instead of a centre where it takes place."

He was referring of course to the degrading international criminal recognition of the Vancouver Model!

I heard the Attorney-General had a copy of my cynical novel on the subject, *Laundering the Dragon. Black Renminbi.* Renminbi is the Communist Chinese name for their currency.

Towards the end of January 2022, I was honoured when the very tall, serious and attentive politician joined me in a pub lunch to talk about the book, money-laundering, and my thoughts for possible solutions regarding the housing industry.

I felt confident enough to chat with him about real estate policy, after all, my entire life had been in the property business. I had sat on the Vancouver Mayor's housing commission and was a long-time director of one of Western Canada's largest high-rise apartment builders.

But with respect money crime and laundering in the real estate business, all I could do, in common with others, was commiserate at the lack of hard information, or any sign of determination by the federal government to act.

Pity I had nothing to offer him regarding gambling!

It had long been known that the money services business needed regulating; that obviously deeply involved banks, accountants and lawyers must come clean about their dubious clients; that luxury goods cash sales were criminally out of control; that residents and people in business blithely evaded taxes; that the controversial civil forfeiture might be more widely used; and that unexplained wealth should be questioned.

He was forcefully raising the issue and expected the Cullen Inquiry to lay out a plan of action. But money-laundering itself could not exist until the precedent crime establishing the money as dirty had been successfully and legally litigated.

There would be no point in extensive provincial action until the Federal Government itself had been induced to do its duty and take determined and fully budgeted action against persistent money crime in Canada. This is still not happening.

And while we just shrug, our national business ethics continue to crumble and the offshore previously Empire countries continue to prosper.

David Eby had Cullen's Report to guide him as he assumed the supreme powers of Premier to do something about the appalling situation. But without knowledgeable, dedicated and fully budgeted Federal action against money crime, there is frankly little he can do.

How could he trace money while so many of my previous Empire countries were actively engaged in hiding it!

As we parted after our lunch, he asked tactfully if I was writing another book. When I said it would be about 'Celebrities who have met me' he laughed.

"That is a great title," he said. So here it is!

Covid superstar Penny Ballam

Dr Penny Ballam OBC, was already enjoying a remarkable career long before Covid disrupted all our lives and projected her into super-stardom.

She had previously managed the entire British Columbia health system as Deputy Minister of Health and when Covid struck in January 2020, she was Chair of the central Vancouver Coastal Heath Authority. All along, she has been a clinical professor of medicine at the University of British Columba, specialising in hematology and bone marrow transplant.

Her life-long prestigious medical and management career suited her perfectly for the dramatic public service that was coming her way.

Lane and I had fortunately travelled extensively because all travel screeched to a halt. We had a trans-Australia train trip and some big upper West Coast whale sharks all booked up to be scuba-ed, early in 2020. Then the entire world changed.

'Wuhan' came forcibly into our lives and the panic for the literally lifesaving Covid vaccinations began.

That was when our friend *Dr Penny Ballam* stepped up and with her expert small team, provided a most remarkably efficient and timely Covid vaccine roll-out for British Columbia. She was fortuitously Chair of Coastal Health, which had her in place for the first Covid case in British Columbia in January 2020. And then she organised the remarkable vaccination roll-out just over a year later.

Their success, together with that of the entire medical staff, led by veteran health minister *Hon. Adrian Dix* and the tireless, remarkably calm *Dr Bonnie Henry OBC* saved countless lives; possibly ours. Now that is well earned super-celebrity!

Lane and I got to know *Penny* and *Marian* early in the century when she enjoyed a brief non-conflicted time and was able to join several prestigious boards, including Bentall Capital, of which I was Chair at the time.

Like Lane, Penny had grown up in Westmount, Montreal and graduated initially from McGill University. She continued her education in the States and then completed her medical specialty at the University of British Columbia.

After running our medical system, Penny moved on to undertake a remarkably difficult, different job as Vancouver City Manager which she endured for seven years, way out of her medical field.

On her retirement from that endeavour, *Vancouver Mayor Gregor Robertson* described her as "a force of nature, brilliant and very capable".

* * *

We all faced our personal anxieties, isolation and problems during Covid. But it finally passed, and with that crisis over, Penny could return to new special challenges, now as Health Advocate to the British Columbia *Premier David Eby.*

And the world could return to its quarrelsome normality.

Prince Philip

His Royal Highness Prince Philip came to Canada many times, so it is reasonable that he, of all celebrities, would bump into me eventually.

He often turned up for his Duke of Edinburgh Awards dinners, which I attended. But it was unexpected when the Prince got quite so close to me.

In 1986 he had come to Vancouver to promote his World Wildlife Fund (which he had insensitively founded the year he shot the tiger in India!) He had in fact met me before in 1969 at one of his Duke of Edinburgh Award lunches, so I was somewhat disappointed he did not immediately say, "Hello John".

But he nodded greeting and said, "What is going on?" rolling his eyes but grinning at the commotion. We had been pushed together into an elevator taking us from our drinks reception to the ballroom where his presentation would take place. He was smiling to see his two frantic, burley security guys fighting in vain to get through the crowd to protect him. Then the doors slid shut.

He was chatty and relaxed in the elevator.

He always looked supremely comfortable in Canada, but about a decade later he appeared decidedly tense appearing in Hong Kong.

Philip had first visited Hong Kong immediately after the World War, as a young acting naval officer, and it must have been galling to be sent by the Queen to hand her territory to Communist China half a century later, further depleting her holdings.

* * *

The original Scottish opium drug dealers and the British naval and military power had admittedly simply taken Hong Kong by force from a China previously weakened by its own persistent corruption and drug use in the mid-1800s.

It was indeed originally just a barren, pretty much deserted rock, but after a century and a half of exploiting it at great profit, the Empire found it hard to give up. But China was offering cheap trade and was persuasive.

It had not helped the Empire's slipping image when Prime Minister Margaret Thatcher ignominiously made a spectacle of herself by falling down the ceremonial steps when she went to China to negotiate.

Mao Tse-tung had nevertheless signed the fifty-year, Sino-British Joint Declaration, setting up a special administration area with a separate economic and governing system from China's. He still needed Hong Kong as a contact with the West and the deal at the time suited everyone.

In a shining white British naval uniform in 1997, the be-meddled Prince Philip said he was proud of the rights and freedoms Britain had provided to Hong Kong. Britain would continue a close association with Hong Kong which continued to share the English common law. Optimistic observations indeed!

He assured the assembly, with a firm voice, "This is not goodbye."

* * *

Flags had been run down, and then new ones run up, bands had played, and China was back! But it became obvious Hong Kong's days were limited as the glistening high-rise Shanghai progressively increased its international financial prominence and China dramatically imposed its influence around the world.

* * *

An exploratory trip we took in 2012 on the exciting new high-speed rail link between Beijing and the already fabled modern financial city of Shanghai had demonstrated China's apparent shining new modern efficiency to us.

Significantly we then found Hong Kong nestling in a Guangdong Province approaching a hundred million in population. And that an incredibly ambitious bridge/tunnel project had been commenced to link Hong Kong to the mainland.

China was ploughing back a very high percentage of national growth into infrastructure and housing rather than distributing earnings to create new industry and increase employment, which would bring future economic strife and political concern for them.

* * *

When we returned before Covid the bridge to Macao had opened but Hong Kong was actively embroiled in civil resistance and protests, which had started with the Umbrella Movement in 2014.

The trouble got going when the Sanding Committee in China dictated the autocratic way in which Hong Kong was to be ruled in the future, under the 'amended' Joint Agreement. Changes were obviously progressively removing personal freedoms and Hong Kong was subjected to their assertive Communist Party rule.

From then we have avoiding travel to Hong Kong for political and safety reasons. But, anyway, from Wuhan, came Covid.

***

In *Laundering the Dragon* the daughter of our Chinese-Canadian heroine has gone to Hong Kong to support the Umbrella Protest. She argues with her 'auntie' Ah-Cy who is a senior member of the Communist Party. She tearfully states:

"China is one of the most brutal, totalitarian states anywhere, denying human rights and now beginning to impose its awful control on free people around the entire world. It is finally dawning on us, even our profiteers, that this must be stopped.

"And talking of profiteers how is it that in a Communist country your political leaders and their families, like you, are some of the richest people in the world? Your internet generation in China will one day demand answers and their quest for freedom of expression will then change your system."

She finished with a smirk, speaking Cantonese, "It is easier to dam a river than silence the voice of the people."

Ah-Cy was shocked by hearing such heresy spoken so openly. "Hong Kong only contains seven million people, part of a hundred million in Guangdong. You will obviously not be allowed to confront the entire Chinese system in this way, so why all the fuss? The wealthy people and big companies are supporting China anyway for profit. You must lose!"

Cathie jumped up, waving her umbrella angrily. They heard her exiting, singing the stirring Glory to Hong Kong *protest song loudly and defiantly.*

Now you will be arrested for singing such songs as *Glory to Hong Kong*. And those defiant young voices have been forcibly silenced.

The free-speaking folks of Hong Kong, a territory previously accessible to all, will just disappear into the morass of dehumanising Communist control.

Prince Philip had it wrong. It really was "Goodbye, Hong Kong." Just as it was a Goodbye to the Empire when the Queen had admitted in one of her Addresses to the Nation "We are no longer a Sovereign Power."

Queen of a Lost Empire

It had come as just another shock to the remaining Empire in 2021, when, still masked and under the threat of Covid, Barbados decided it finally had enough of Royal Families and with a sunny ceremony became its latest casualty.

This was even more final however, because they had been independent since 1966 but were now becoming a republic, still in the financially advantageous Commonwealth of course, but free of the Crown.

Celebrity singer Rihanna was the star in many ways at the ceremony appearing as a national hero, while protectively masked Prince Charles looked understandably glum, losing such a splendid island after 400 years of ownership. Also, for him to surrender the limelight to the visibly outstanding Bajan rock star, Rihanna Fenty, speaks volumes for modern interests!

So many changes, but the tourists still arrive, and *Bajan Ram Edgehill* still takes out his diving boat *Scotch 'n' Soda* and pours the rum liberally as before.

* * *

Sigh. Poor Charles. With all these spoilsports going their own way, that left sadly few territories for him to inherit: the Cayman Islands and Bermuda, (with only about 65,000 residents each, but lots of tourists,) Anguilla, Barbuda, Montserrat, Turks and Caicos Islands, Gibraltar, British Virgin Islands, Tristan da Cunha, and a dozen prominent but even smaller territories. All waiting to declare their independence when the time is right!

Dissipating the inherent wealth, accumulated by a rapacious Empire, is a slow business but it is now catching up more quickly with the United Kingdom. The British came up with a remarkable formula benefitting from abundant coal and inventiveness at the beginning of the industrial revolution. At the time the industrialists had abundant cheap labour at home and as countries were annexed, they plundered cheap raw materials. British products achieved their manufacturing and trading monopoly.

Protected by military might, and participating politicians, enormous concentrations of wealth resulted, leading to more industrial expansion and so on, while the monopolistic Empire lasted. Now times have changed dramatically for the United Kingdom and new circumstances favour other rising dynasties.

Brexit was a forlorn attempt by the traditional English Empire loyalists to revive the past dreams of Imperialism, but which instead seems to have further isolated their shrinking influence and economy.

To a considerable, and unethical extent, the break-up of the Empire has provided the financial City of London with a replacing source of income, managing unrecorded capital for the invisible wealthy of the world.

Many of its previous colonial territories now serve to conceal the notorious 'offshore' investment market and together with America, the United Kingdom is recognised as a prime protector of international money crime and provider of laundering services.

***

Despite the negative things I have expressed about the Empire, Her Majesty Queen Elizabeth remained high in my own affection and respect.

I always felt a personal connection. She was less than ten years older, and as a youngster I remember seeing movies showing her serving in uniform during the war, as a friendly young ambulance driver.

Then while I was just a teenager, she rushed back from Kenya upset at her father's unexpected death and to become my Queen.

In her colony of Hong Kong, we gathered during Christmas to hear her annual message to the nation, and she always managed to maintain a personal contact with her subjects. At least that is what I felt personally.

I was certainly sad when she died in September 2022. We had reached an end together. There will be no more Children of the Empire!

Now we have a King, Charles the Third, *of Canada.*

After Charles and Camilla's marriage, when he was still Prince of Wales, on one of their several visits to Canada, Lane and I were invited to a reception in Vancouver to be graced by the royal couple.

"I have no intention of attending or risking meeting them, after the terrible way they treated my Diana," Lane stated firmly.

Which is why, despite my life of service to Queen Elizabeth, His Majesty Charles the Third, by the Grace of God, of the United Kingdom, of Great Britain and Northern Ireland and his other Disappearing Realms and Territories, King, Head of the Commonwealth, Defender of the Faith … has failed to meet me.

* * *

The ancient half-timbered family home is still there in England but now a renovated showpiece, like much of the country. The quiet market town of Sudbury is the same as it has been for centuries. Memories of Hitler and the German bombardment have long faded.

The grandeur of the Empire itself has come and gone. Almost a thousand years of fabled conquest and colonisation are over, and the Children of the Empire can relax back into their pubs and rose-covered cottages in their 'green and pleasant land,' just dreaming of those grand old days, when England ruled.

Main territories that gained complete independence from the British Empire:

Normandy 1450, Calais 1558, USA 1776, Minorca 1802, Canada 1867 (conclusively in 1982!), Heligoland 1890, Australia 1901 (1986), New Zealand 1906 (1947).

First World War 1914-1918:

Afghanistan 1919, Ireland 1922, Egypt 1922, Iraq 1932.

During the period of the book Second World War 1939-1945:

Jordan 1946, India 1947, New Zealand 1947, Israel 1948, Myanmar 1948, Sri Lanka 1948, Libya 1951, Muscat and Oman 1951, Sudan 1956, Ghana 1957, Malaya 1957, British Cameroon 1960, Cyprus 1960, Lagos 1960, Nigeria 1960, Somali 1960, Togoland 1960, Kuwait 1961, Sierra Leone 1961, Tanganyika 1961, Jamaica 1962, Samoa 1962, Trinidad and Tobago 1962, Uganda 1962, Aden 1963, Sarawak 1963, Singapore 1963, Zanzibar 1963, Kenya 1963, Malawi 1964, Malta 1964, Zambia 1964, Gambia 1965, Maldives 1965, Rhodesia 1965, Barbados 1966, Basutoland 1966, Botswana 1966, Guyana 1966, Lesotho 1966, Aden 1967, Yemen 1967, Eswatini 1968, Mauritius 1968, Nauru 1968, Swaziland 1968, Fiji 1970, Tonga 1970, Bahrain 1971, United Arab Emirates 1971, Qatar 1971, Bahamas 1973, Grenada 1974, Dominica 1978, Seychelles 1976, Solomon Islands 1978, Tuvalu 1978, Gilbert Islands 1979, St, Lucia 1979, St Vincent 1979, Antigua and Barbuda 1981, Belize 1981, Canada 1982, Saint Kitts and Nevis 1983, Brunei 1984, Australia 1986, Hong Kong 1997.

Territories still under British influence:

Anguilla, Bermuda, British Antarctic Territory, British Indian Ocean Territory, British Virgin Islands, Cayman Islands, Falkland Islands, Gibraltar, Montserrat, Pitcairn, Saint Helena, Tristan da Cunha, Turks and Caicos Islands.

Acknowledgments

Producing a book is absolutely a team effort.

This is the third time I have the pleasure of sincerely thanking celebrity Australian editor Kevin McDonald for offering to design the layout, and edit a book I have written. Lane and I were fortunate to become friends with Kevin and his wife Pat in beautiful Noosa on the East Coast of Australia. They are related to the late surgeon Dr Willy Jones, a hero of this narrative.

The striking cover is the painstaking artistic work of Emily Rose who has helped us previously and this time took on the entire cover design.

Our ever-patient publisher, through his Adagio Media, continues our lawyer son, Bob D'Eith KC. He is indeed also a Child of the Empire having been born in the Colony of Hong Kong, but featuring in the book in his Canadian role as a Member of the Legislative Assembly of British Columbia.

Our promotion expert in Singapore remains on-line expert and nephew Oliver Mallich, who waits to spring into action upon publication.

You will have gathered from the narrative that Lane and I are very close. She has played a particularly supportive part in our literary adventures around the world and patiently rereads manuscripts in addition to her own very active life.

The opinions and mistakes are all mine, but I acknowledge the essential and practical part our team plays in these ventures. I very much appreciate everyone's personal support.

John D'Eathe, West Vancouver,
in a finally, fully independent Canada.

Made in the USA
Columbia, SC
06 October 2024